Government and Society in Nineteenth-Century Britain
Commentaries on British Parliamentary Papers

MONETARY AND FINANCIAL POLICY

By the same authors:

F. W. FETTER:

Monetary Inflation in Chile (Princeton University Press, 1931)
The Irish Pound (Allen and Unwin, 1955)
The Economic Writings of Francis Horner (Ed.) (The London School of Economics and Political Science, 1957)
Selected Economic Writings of Thomas Attwood (Ed.) (London School of Economics and Political Science, 1964)
Development of British Monetary Orthodoxy (Harvard University Press, 1965)

P. FORD

The Economics of Collective Bargaining (Blackwell, Oxford, 1958)
Social Theory and Social Practice (Irish University Press, 1968)

P. & G. FORD

Hansard's Catalogue and Breviate of Parliamentary Papers, 1696-1834 (IUP British Parliamentary Papers, General Indexes, Volume 1)
Select List of British Parliamentary Papers, 1833-99 (Irish University Press, 1969)
A Breviate of Parliamentary Papers, 1900-16 (Irish University Press, 1969)
A Breviate of Parliamentary Papers, 1917-39 (Irish University Press, 1969)
A Breviate of Parliamentary Papers, 1940-54 (Irish University Press, 1970)
Luke Graves Hansard's Diary, 1814-41 (Blackwell, Oxford, 1962)

P. & G. FORD AND DIANA MARSHALLSEY

Select List of British Parliamentary Papers, 1955-64 (Irish University Press, 1970)

D. GREGORY

Statistics for Business Studies (McGraw-Hill, 1967)
A History of Death Duties (D. C. Heath, forthcoming)

Government and Society in Nineteenth-Century Britain
Commentaries on British Parliamentary Papers

MONETARY AND FINANCIAL POLICY

Frank W. Fetter

Derek Gregory

Introduction by P. and G. Ford

IRISH UNIVERSITY PRESS

u
26·5
80

7 7 35 11

IRISH UNIVERSITY PRESS

Irish University Press British Parliamentary Papers Series
CHIEF EDITORIAL ADVISERS
P. Ford
Professor Emeritus, Southampton University
Mrs. G. Ford

Government and Society in Nineteenth-Century Britain Series
EDITOR
J. Friedmann

ISBN 0 7165 2217 9 (case bound) 0 7165 2218 7 (paper bound)

All forms of micro-publishing
© Irish University Microforms

Printed in Great Britain by
The Whitefriars Press Ltd., London and Tonbridge.

101204

Contents

Abbreviations

C., Cd., Cmd.	Command Paper	mins. of ev.	minutes of evidence
Ch.	Chairman	q. (qq.)	question(s)
ev.	evidence	R. Com.	Royal Commission
HC	House of Commons	Rep.	Report
HL	House of Lords	Sel. Cttee.	Select Committee

Citations

The form used for House and Command papers is:

> session/paper no./volume no./volume page no.

Example:

> 1845(602)xii,331 or 1845(602)XII,331

If the title has not been given in the text, the form should be preceded by the title and description:

> title and description/session/paper no./volume no./volume page no.

Examples:

> Game Law. Sel. Cttee. Rep.; 1845(602)xii,331
> London Squares. R.Com. Rep.; 1928-29 Cmd. 3196,viii,111

References are to the *House of Commons* bound sets, *except* where the paper is in the House of Lords set only. From this it follows:

a. Where the paper is the report of a Lords select committee (communicated to the Commons) it must be marked HL to indicate this and to distinguish it from a Commons select committee:

Example:

> Sale of Beer. Sel.Cttee.HL. Rep.; 1850(398)xviii,483.

b. Where the paper is in the Lords papers only, HL should be added to the paper number. This can be done in the form HL(259) or (HL.259).

c. For a reference to a statement on a particular page of a paper, the title and description should be followed by the *printed* page number of the paper:

> title etc./printed page no./session/paper no./volume no./vol. page no.

Example:

> Finance and Industry. Cttee.Rep.p.134;1930-31Cmd.3897,xiii,219

Where the reference is to the Irish University Press series the citation is:

> IUP/subject/title/volume no.

Example:

> IUP Monetary Policy: General 4.

Introduction to Parliamentary Papers

P. and G. Ford

A fully comprehensive definition of parliamentary papers would include all those which form part of the necessary machinery of parliamentary government, even those concerned with the procedures of the day-to-day business. But from the point of view of the researcher three groups are of primary importance. The first group, the Journals, record the things done in parliament. The second group, the Debates, record the things said in parliament (the publication of the House of Commons Debates became known as Hansard throughout the world and was at first not an official but a private venture receiving public subsidy). The third group, Papers arising in or presented to parliament deal with the formulation, development and execution of its policy. It is to this third group, for many years known as 'Blue Books' because of the blue paper with which most of them were covered, that the name Parliamentary Papers became particularly attached.

After 1801 the papers were gathered together and bound in two separate sessional sets, one for the House of Commons and the other for the House of Lords. These volumes include reports of select committees, composed of a limited number of members of either House appointed to examine particular problems, and reports of royal commissions and committees of enquiry appointed in form by the Crown though on the advice of ministers of by ministers themselves. These latter have the double advantage of comprising persons from outside the House thought to be experts on the subjects in hand, persons prominent in public affairs or representative of some body of opinion, experience or interest, and of not being limited in their work to the length of a parliamentary session. All these bodies reported the results of their enquiries together with the evidence taken to the authority which appointed them. The reports of select committees and the papers which departments were required by Act to send to parliament, because they originated *in* the House were grouped into a numbered series as House Papers. Royal commissions reported formally to the Crown—even submitting massive volumes of evidence for it to read—and committees reported to the minister concerned. Because these were the work of bodies *outside* the House, the papers were brought to the House and incorporated in the Sessional Papers through the use of an historic formula which embodies much of the development of constitutional monarchy, 'Presented by Command'.

It was these committees and commissions which uncovered the evils of the work of children in factories and mines, the evils of bad housing and sanitation and of inadequate water supply in the new sprawling towns created by the Industrial Revolution, as well as the difficulties relating to monetary policy and the new phenomenon of recurrent trade depressions. The witnesses brought before the enquiring bodies included the victims of the new industrial conditions–little children who had worked in factories and mines, the exploited immigrants in the sweated trades, and the leaders of the early efforts to unionize workmen, such as John Gast in 1815, John Doherty in 1838 and the whole of the top leadership of the great trade unions in 1867-9. What is more remarkable is that the oral evidence was printed verbatim. Even Marx was impressed by the commissions' plenary powers for getting at the truth, the competence and freedom from partisanship and respect of persons displayed by the English Factory Inspectors, the Medical Officers reporting on public health and the Commissioners of Enquiry into the exploitation of women and children, into housing and food. There is no parallel in the world for such a series of searching and detailed enquiries covering so long a span of years and embracing every phase of the transition from a rural aristocratic society to an industrialized democracy. It is the most significant of these reports on a century of investigation, the 'policy papers', that are embodied in the Irish University Press series.

The method of personal examination of witnesses had occasionally to be modified when central hearings were not practicable. Before the Benthemite conception of a unified central and local government machine had been realized in practice, the central authorities often knew little of what was going on in the localities. The many thousands of parishes administered the poor laws in their own ways so that the *Royal Commission on the Poor Laws* (1834) had to send round assistant commissioners to carry out and report on a detailed standardized plan of enquiry. The *Royal Commission on Municipal Corporations* (1835) had to make district enquiries on how the boroughs and 'places claiming to be boroughs' conducted their affairs. The effect of adverse forces on agriculture could be country-wide: the *Royal Commission on the Depressed Condition of the Agricultural Interests* (1881-2), on *Agricultural Depression* (1894-7) and the *Labour Commission* (1892-4) looking into agricultural labour, each made use of assistant commissioners to find out what was common and what was different in the problems of the various districts. These papers are a mine of information.

There are also the various famous reports by great civil servants, such as Horner's on the enforcement of factory legislation, Tremenheere's on the state of the mining districts, bound in the sets under the heading of commissioners' reports, and Southwood Smith's on the *Physical Causes of Sickness and Mortality to which the Poor are Exposed*, tucked away in an appendix to an annual report.

Two aspects of these investigations—the membership of the committees and the importance of British constitutional procedure—are worthy of note. The fullness and considerable integrity of these penetrating investigations were remarkable in that in the first half of the century the members of the committees and commissions which made them were not, as they would be today, drawn from or representative of the great bodies of the working classes. On the contrary, they were from the wealthy and ruling groups, for the composition of the House of Commons reflected the fact that even after the Reform Act of 1832 the number of voters was still but a tiny fraction of the adult population. The Northcote-Trevelyan proposals for the reform of the civil service, by replacing recruitment by patronage with open competition, were approved by a cabinet all of whom, said Gladstone, who was a member of it, were more aristocratic than himself. No doubt they had their blind sides. For most of the century they assumed the existing class structure without much question; and there were fields in which their approach to problems and the conclusions they drew were influenced not only by the prevalent social philosophies, but class ideals and interests, as in the investigations into trade unions, game laws, etc. But the facts elicited in the examination of witnesses were not covered up or hidden—because apart from pressure by reforming groups, the constitutional procedure was that reports and evidence should be submitted and printed verbatim.

Further groups of papers are those which arose from the expansion of Britain overseas to control widely scattered colonial possessions and the development of areas of white settlement, Canada, Australia, and New Zealand. At the outset both kinds of territories were in some degree controlled from Whitehall. On the latter, beside formal committees of enquiry, there was a mass of despatches to and correspondence with colonial governors on the opening and sales of land for settlement, taxation, the administration of justice and the slow replacement of central control by primitive local representative bodies which eventually became the parliaments of self-governing dominions. In the case of the colonial possessions, after the Act abolishing slavery had been passed, the most striking feature was the immense body of papers which offer unique insight into the problem of enforcing this new political principle in widely scattered territories, differing in climate, crop conditions, land tenure, the character and importance of slavery and in social structure. These are revealed in an immense volume of despatches, correspondence and instructions issued by the Colonial Office and the Foreign Office to colonial governors and their little Assemblies, which offered varying degrees of co-operation and resistance, and by the Admiralty in orders to commanders of naval vessels engaged all over the world in efforts to suppress the slave trade.

The great body of material for the nineteenth century occupies some 7,000 official folio volumes. At the outset the problem of making it available had to be met by the Printer to the House of Commons, Luke Hansard, who kept it in stock and numbered the House papers. He was frequently asked by M.P.s and others for sets of existing papers on particular questions then under discussion in the House or by the public. This led him to take two steps. He made special collections of papers arranged in subject order, and prepared a series of indexes to the papers, some in subject and some in alphabetical order. But the passage of a century has enlarged the number of papers to be handled and the scale of the problems; and at the same time we now have to meet the demand not only of the politician concerned with the problems of his time, but those of professional historians and researchers ranging over the whole century.

To deal with the papers on Home Affairs the Fords' *Select List of British Parliamentary Papers 1833-99* includes 4,000 policy papers arranged in subject order, so that researchers can follow the development lines of policy easily through any collection of papers. But complete collections are few and far between and even ample ones not common. The Irish University Press Parliamentary Papers series supplies this deficiency first by reprinting all the major policy papers, comveniently brought together in subject sets, e.g. 32 volumes on Agriculture, 44 volumes on Industrial Relations, 15 volumes on Children's Employment, 55 volumes on Education, and so on. Secondly, it has retained what was the great virtue of the original enquiries by reprinting with the reports all the volumes of evidence. Thirdly, in those fields where despatches, correspondence and instructions are vital as in the case of the papers on slavery, Canada, Australia, New Zealand, as far as possible all the papers on these matters found in the British Parliamentary series have been reprinted, e.g. 94 volumes on Slavery, 36 on Canada, 34 on Australia.

The series includes the most commonly used official general alphabetical indexes from which researchers can trace papers referred to in the footnotes of scholarly works and in the references in parliamentary reports themselves. In addition to the official indexes, a special index[1] to the 1,000 volumes has been prepared which will also provide cross references, so that the official indexes can be used either with the official sessional sets of with the IUP reprints.

1   *Checklist of British Parliamentary Papers in the Irish University Press 1000-Volume Series 1801-1899* (Shannon: 1972). See also p. 000.

MONETARY POLICY

Frank W. Fetter

6

Contents

MONETARY POLICY

2**Commentary**

8

The Documents

Bibliography

Commentary *

The Context

For a period of over a hundred years, from the outbreak of the Napoleonic wars until the last decade of the nineteenth century, Great Britain was engaged in an almost continuous debate on monetary and banking policy and on the operation of its financial institutions. The debate produced numerous books and a wealth of brochures, countless letters to newspapers and many periodical articles. The latter were mostly anonymous, starting with the founding of the *Edinburgh Review* in 1802, and then the *Quarterly Review* (1809), *Blackwood's Edinburgh Magazine* (1817), *Westminster Review* (1824), *Fraser's Magazine* (1830) and *The Economist* (1844). The parliamentary debates as reported in Hansard (and sometimes more fully in *Mirror of Parliament* for the years 1828-41) gave, at the political level, a blow by blow account of most of these controversies. However, the most continuous and extended record, both of the facts of economic changes, and of opinions as to the causes of these changes and as to the actions that government should take to correct abuses, is in the British parliamentary papers. With one exception, every major financial disturbance for nearly a century, beginning in 1793, was followed by the appointment of a select or secret committee, the collection of information, the examination of witnesses, and the presentation of a report, frequently recommending or opposing legislative changes. Only in the case of the Overend-Gurney panic of 1866, the last of the three occasions before the Great War that the Bank Act of 1844 was suspended, was there no parliamentary post mortem to fill in, for economist and historian, the details of the crisis. In no country up to 1914 has the inquisitive spirit of legislatures left such a wealth of documentation on the monetary and banking problems of an emerging industrial-finance society.

Developments in the French War—1793-96

The outbreak of the war with France in February 1793 followed decades of quiescence in monetary and banking controversy.[1] The action of the government in 1717, largely on the advice of Sir Isaac Newton, of fixing the value of the guinea at 21 shillings, in effect established a gold-silver

* I am indebted to Mr. Keith Horsefield and to Professor R. S. Sayers for constructive criticism of an earlier draft of this commentary.

[1] A fuller discussion of the British monetary and banking situation before the Napoleonic wars is given in F. W. Fetter, *Development of British Monetary Orthodoxy 1793-1875,* Chapter I, 'The Monetary and Banking World of 1797' (Cambridge, Mass.: Harvard University Press, 1965); of the Irish situation in F. W. Fetter, *The Irish Pound* (London: Allen and Unwin; and Evanston, Illinois: Northwestern University Press, 1955), pp. 9-12.

mint ratio of 15.21 : 1. This gave Britain a *de facto* gold standard, as the market ratio of gold to silver was below 15.21 : 1 most of the time until the 1790s. It meant that it was not profitable to bring silver to the mint for coinage and, as the ratio unfavourable to silver continued, all but the most degraded silver coin went to the melting pot. The Bank of England, established in 1694, was the only chartered bank in England; Scotland had three chartered banks—the Bank of Scotland, the Royal Bank of Scotland, and the British Linen Bank; Ireland had one, the Bank of Ireland, chartered in 1783. The remaining banks were all private. Monetary circulation consisted of gold coin; notes of private banks, which generally had only a local circulation; notes of the chartered banks, with those of Scotland and Ireland circulating only in their respective countries, and those of the Bank of England having no general circulation outside of London; clipped and badly worn silver coins; and a miscellaneous assortment of copper coins. All banks redeemed their notes in gold; or in the case of English private banks in notes of the Bank of England, and in the case of Scottish and Irish private banks in notes of the chartered banks of those countries. Notes of the chartered banks were not legal tender, but in practice they were almost universally accepted on the same basis as gold.

Figures on the relative importance of deposit and cheque payments before the 1790s are not available, but apparently deposit banking was on a quite limited scale, and cheque payments were confined largely to sums of £25 or more. Private banks were subject to no special banking legislation, but only to the general laws that applied to all business. The Bank of England and the other chartered banks were governed by the special terms of their charters, but in no case were there any reserve requirements against either notes or deposits. British legislation forbade the export of British coin, or of specie from melted-down British coin. However, both because of a floating supply of foreign coin and specie, and because of violations of British law, the exchange rates between Britain and foreign countries moved much as they would have had there been no restrictions on the export of the precious metals.[2]

Most of the continent of Europe, and in particular Hamburg, with which a large amount of the British foreign exchange was carried on,[3] was on a silver standard. Hence, even if the restriction on melting and support

2 Discussed by the author in more detail in *Development of British Monetary Orthodoxy*, pp. 4-6.

3 Practically all the foreign exchange operations of Britain and Ireland were carried on through London. There is a mention in the 1797 hearings of some direct exchange relations of Ireland with Portugal—presumably in connection with imports of port—but apparently they were quantitatively insignificant. There may have been direct exchange relations between Scottish cities and the Continent, but I know of no reference to them.

of British coin had had no effect on exchange rates, there would have been
fluctuations in the London-Hamburg rate greater than if both countries
had been on a gold standard. But in view of the relative stability of the
gold-silver ratio in Hamburg—the highest yearly average between 1775 and
1789 was 14 : 92, the lowest 14 : 42, and in 1790-96 the highest annual
average was 15 : 65, the lowest 15 : 00—the existence of two standards
had only a minor effect on the exchanges. There was, of course, a shifting
par of exchange between London and Hamburg, but shifts in the par,
particularly in any period of only a few months, were generally less than
the fluctuations around that par due to balance of payments influence.
Even so, much of contemporary discussion of exchange rate fluctuations
in the Restriction years 1797-1821 is confusing, particularly to the reader
of today, because it is not always clear whether the fluctuations were due
to a shifting par or to fluctuations around that par.

The first three years of war brought only one major problem for the
British monetary and banking system: a financial panic with widespread
bankruptcies of both banks and commercial houses that followed a few
weeks after the outbreak of war. Despite the close time sequence between
the outbreak of war and the crisis, it is probable that the major causes
antedated the war, and all the war did was to determine the timing of the
crisis.[4] The crisis initiated a controversy that was settled only after some
80 years by the general acceptance of what came to be known as the
Bagehot doctrine: the responsibility of the Bank of England to support the
credit structure in time of crisis. Up to the 1790s the Bank of England
was, in the words of Adam Smith, 'the greatest bank of circulation in
Europe', and 'a great engine of state', but there was virtually no discussion
of its role in holding the nation's ultimate banking reserves, or its
responsibility to support the money market in time of crisis. This is not
surprising, as banking and credit played a relatively smaller role in the
nation's economy, and financial crises were much more limited in scale
and less serious in their effects on the whole economy than in the
following century. But regardless of the absence of any theory about the
need to support the money market in time of crisis, or the lack of
precedents for such action, the events of 1793 called for some action to
support the crisis-ridden markets. Although quantitative data are limited,
the Bank granted credit in a way that suggests some recognition of a
responsibility to prevent financial collapse.[5] But whatever aid the Bank

4 This is the judgement of Thomas Tooke, *A History of Prices*, I (London: 1838),
pp. 176-77. More details on the crisis and the action by the Bank of England and by
the government are given in Fetter, *Development of British Monetary Orthodoxy*,
pp. 12-16.
5 Sir John Clapham, *The Bank of England. A History* (Cambridge: Cambridge
University Press, 1945), I, pp. 260-65, and F. W. Fetter, *Development of British
Monetary Orthodoxy*, pp. 12-16.

granted did not stem the crisis, and the question then arose in parliament as to whether the Bank should be required to grant further aid, or whether aid should come directly from the government. The House of Commons appointed a *Select Committee . . . to take into Consideration the Present State of Commercial Credit,* whose report (IUP Monetary Policy: General 1) is the earliest of any report in the 31 volumes here surveyed. The committee, after hearings, recommended the issue of Exchequer bills by a board of commissioners against the collateral of goods or personal securities. The bill was passed, but not without some statements, in the Commons and in the Lords, that in time of crisis it was the duty of the Bank of England rather than the government to support the market.

Causes of exchange rate fluctuations

The Bank of England and the Bank of Ireland suspended specie payments early in 1797, and until legislation in 1819, which led to the resumption of payments in 1821, the most important single topic of parliamentary debate and of parliamentary investigation in the monetary field was the causes of the suspension of payments by the banks, and the actions necessary to maintain exchange rate stability. The main decisions had been reached by 1819, but echoes of the controversy, and occasional challenges of the decisions reached, continued through the 1840s.

Despite heavy foreign expenditures by Britain, including subsidies, and the transfer of the Austrian loans in the early years of the war, there was no depreciation of the foreign exchanges, or rise in the price of the precious metals, beyond the limits that had prevailed in years of peace. Beginning late in 1795 the Bank's reserves fell off almost steadily, partly from internal drains and partly from external payments. In February 1797, following a quickly repulsed landing of the French in Wales, and heavy bank runs, the Bank of England suspended cash payments, as did the Bank of Ireland a few days later.

The suspension was followed by the appointment of secret committees by both the Commons and Lords. Their reports (IUP Monetary Policy: General 1) are important to the economic historian and to the student of monetary theory, not only for factual material on the background of the suspension, but also for the analysis by some witnesses, in particular Henry Thornton[6] on the central role of the Bank of England, and Walter Boyd on the need for the Bank, in the case of an internal run for cash, to ease rather than to restrict credits.

For the first six years of the Restriction, exchange rate fluctuations,

---

6   Thornton's evidence was reprinted in 1939 by F. A. v.Hayek, in his reprint of Thornton's *Paper Credit of Great Britain* (London: Allen and Unwin), pp. 279-310.

both between Dublin and London, and between London and the Continent, were, except for a few months, but little greater than had been the case before the suspension of cash payments. A brief depreciation of the Hamburg exchange in 1800, together with rising commodity prices, produced a flurry of controversy, which had its focus in Walter Boyd's booklet of early 1801, *A Letter to the Right Honourable William Pitt, on the Influence of the Stoppage of Issues in Specie at the Bank of England; on the Prices of Provisions, and other Commodities,* in which Boyd put forth forcibly a primarily monetary explanation of price changes and exchange rate fluctuations. The controversy subsided as exchange rates returned close to their pre-suspension levels; and no parliamentary committees were appointed. In 1802, when exchange rates were no longer a pressing public problem, appeared Henry Thornton's classic, *The Paper Credit of Great Britain,* which, rather than a polemic, was a judicious survey of the problem of exchange rate fluctuations and of the Bank of England's role in the British banking system.

Only in 1803 did the monetary situation once more become the subject of parliamentary investigation. Although the London-Hamburg exchange rate and the price of gold in London were again close to their pre-suspension figures, the Irish currency in 1803 had gone to a discount of 10 per cent as measured by the exchange on London. The House of Commons appointed a *Committee on the Circulating Paper, the Specie, and the Current Coin of Ireland; and also, on the Exchange between that Part of the United Kingdom and Great Britain.* The committee held extended hearings, and the evidence and the committee report reviewed the causes of exchange rate depreciation, and measures necessary to maintain exchange rate stability.[7]

This report on the Irish exchange situation has been overshadowed in popular fame and scholarly interest by the more famous Bullion Report of 1810 (IUP Monetary Policy: General 1). But in its subject matter, in the topics covered in the evidence and in its recommendations the Irish Report anticipated a large part of the work of the Bullion Committee. The witnesses presented two opposing views of the causes of exchange rate fluctuations, and of the policy to be followed to limit these fluctuations. Spokesmen for the Bank of Ireland and several other witnesses presented an essentially 'balance of payments' explanation: monetary policy had no influence on the exchange rates, whose fluctuations were determined by changes in the country's balance of payments, caused by influences other

7 The Report and Minutes of Evidence were printed in 1804 (Sess. 1803-4 [86] vol. 4, p. 1) and reprinted four times as a parliamentary paper. It is not reprinted in the IUP series, but the Report and selections from the Minutes of Evidence are published in F. W. Fetter, *The Irish Pound.*

than monetary policy. This argument was buttressed by support of the 'real bills' doctrine—i.e., that as long as a bank granted credit only on the basis of bills representing business transactions, credit expansion could have no effect on prices or on the exchanges. Other witnesses gave an essentially monetary explanation—often referred to as the Bullionist view—that Irish monetary expansion had been the prime cause of the depreciation of the Irish exchange. The conclusion, specific or implicit, of the second view was that it was possible for the Bank of Ireland, by credit policy and by temporarily drawing on reserves to meet short run situations, to maintain a stable exchange rate.[8] The committee's report, in passages that suggest the hand of Henry Thornton, a member of the committee, in substance supported the second view: that the balance of payments was in large part a reflection of monetary policy, and not an independent exogenous influence on the exchanges.

Almost coincident with the publication of the report, the Dublin-London rate returned close to its old parity, and the London-Hamburg rate remained close to par. These developments quieted the debate, and for the next six years neither pamphleteers nor parliamentary committees concerned themselves with the causes of exchange fluctuations or the actions necessary to maintain a stable exchange. But with the depreciation, late in 1809, of the British pound in terms of the Hamburg exchange, the earlier and short-lived debate over the Irish exchange burst forth on a wider stage. This renewal of the debate was an important chapter in the history of economic thought, for it was the occasion for David Ricardo's debut as an economist, in the form of his three letters to the *Morning Chronicle* on 'The Price of Gold'.[9]

Ricardo expressed in an extreme and dogmatic way the monetary explanation of exchange fluctuations, not making any of the short-run qualifications that holders of the monetary, or Bullionist, position, such as Henry Thornton or T. R. Malthus, were prepared to make. The controversy soon got into the parliamentary arena, when, on a motion of Francis Horner, a young Whig who had written on monetary matters for the *Edinburgh Review,* the Commons appointed the *Select Committee on the High Price of Gold Bullion* (IUP Monetary Policy: General 1), whose report is probably the most famous and widely reprinted of any report of a British parliamentary commission—at least 20 printings in three

8 For a further discussion of these points see F. W. Fetter, *The Irish Pound,* pp. 32-33.
9 For a detailed account of Ricardo's role in this controversy, see *Works and Correspondence of David Ricardo,* Piero Sraffa, ed. (Cambridge: Cambridge University Press, 1951), vol. III, pp. 3-46.

languages.[10] The evidence before the committee, and the report, drafted in large part by Francis Horner, William Huskisson, and Henry Thornton, were in essence an updated version of the proceedings of the Irish Committee of 1804. The spokesmen for the Bank of England, in words that Walter Bagehot later described as 'almost classical by their nonsense', reiterated in even stronger terms the earlier view of the Bank of Ireland—that monetary policy had nothing to do with exchange rates, and that credits on 'real bills', no matter how extensive, could have no inflationary effect. The committee report, however, took the view that the Bank of England policy was the major, although not exclusive, influence on exchange rates, and that appropriate Bank of England policy could maintain a stable rate. The issues of theory and of policy raised by the report were complicated both by British internal politics and by the necessities of wartime finance. Undoubtedly wisely, the Tory government rejected the Bullion Committee's recommendation that cash payments be resumed within two years, even if the war were not over.

The pound continued at a discount in terms of gold, even after Napoleon was safely settled on St. Helena, and the next eight years produced a continuous outpouring of brochures on monetary policy and a wealth of parliamentary oratory. But not until 1819 was there another parliamentary investigation, when both the Commons and the Lords appointed secret committees—the Commons committee under the chairmanship of Robert Peel—to investigate the expediency of the Bank's resuming cash payments.[11] To a large degree the issues were those of the Irish Committee and the Bullion Committee, but in a peacetime setting. The Bank of England witnesses reiterated the views expressed before the Bullion Committee, and the Bank's directors put themselves on record in a resolution transmitted to the Commons committee:

> That this Court cannot refrain from adverting to an opinion, strongly insisted on by some, that the bank has only to reduce its issues to obtain a favourable turn in the exchanges, and a consequent influx of

10 The Printings up to 1955 are listed in my 'The Editions of the Bullion Report' (*Economica*, n.s. XXII, May 1955, pp. 152-57). Since then I have located two Russian reprints of 1941 and 1955, in Russian editions of Ricardo's works, which spread behind the Iron Curtain the once widely held view, to which even Alfred Marshall gave his authority, that Ricardo was one of the authors of the Bullion Report. For a further discussion of the background of the Bullion Report see my 'The Bullion Report Reexamined', *Quarterly Journal of Economics*, LVI, August 1942, pp. 655-65, and reprinted in T. S. Ashton and R. S. Sayers, *Papers on English Monetary History* (Oxford: Clarendon Press, 1953), pp. 66-75; and 'The Politics of the Bullion Report', *Economica*, n.s. XXI, July 1959, pp. 99-120.

11 IUP Monetary Policy: General 2.

the precious metals; the Court conceives it to be its duty to declare, that it is unable to discover any solid foundation for such a sentiment.

But the view, unheeded in the wartime setting, that it was possible to maintain stable exchanges by appropriate monetary policy, had gained increasing strength. The official position of the Bank of England no longer had general acceptance; and even within the Bank there were dissidents who had come to accept the position of Ricardo and of the Bullion Report.[12] The lucid evidence of Ricardo before the two committees contributed to parliamentary support of the Bullionist view. Other factors, outside the narrower orbit of economic analysis, responsible for the change were Robert Peel's view, based primarily on his political conservatism, that the monetary system should have an anchor of stability; increasing public protests against executions for the forgery of Bank of England notes; and a growing hostility in parliament, that transcended party lines, to the Bank of England's authoritarian air.[13]

The committee's proceedings and reports, and the legislation calling for resumption of cash payments and for dropping the prohibition on the melting and export of coin, settled for nearly a hundred years the question of exchange rate stability. Cash payments at the old parity were resumed in 1821. In 1827 the Bank directors rescinded their resolution of 1819 about their inability to control the exchange. From then on there was no concerted challenge, either in the Bank or outside, to the Bank's ability to control exchange rates, although at times the question was raised as to whether the effective control did not come more from the influence of credit policy over short term capital movements than from control over commodity prices. But no parliamentary committee was appointed to review the theory of the Resumption Act of 1819, and in the hearings of 1832 on the Bank Charter Act[14] the Bank directors accepted without question the theory of the Bank's control over exchange rates that little over a decade before they had rejected.

The question of the standard

The Act of 1819 was more than a return to the monetary conditions of 1797. As indicated earlier, in 1797 the British monetary standard was legal bimetallism, as a mint ratio of 15.21 : 1. As this ratio was higher than the market ratio, for over a half century before 1797 Britain had a *de facto*

---

12   J. K. Horsefield, 'The Bankers and the Bullionists in 1819', *Journal of Political Economy*, LVII, October 1949, pp. 442-48, gives a picture of the difference of opinion within the Bank Court.

13 See F. W. Fetter, *Development of British Monetary Orthodoxy*, pp. 71-73, 93-95.

14   IUP Monetary Policy: General 4.

gold standard,[15] subject to the qualification of the prohibition on the export of British gold coin or bullion melted down from British coin. The situation was accepted by the public, with virtually no discussion of the relative merits of bimetallism, a single gold standard, or a single silver standard. In 1794 both the gold-silver ratio in Hamburg and the price of silver in London reached figures at which—eliminating costs involved—it would have been profitable to bring silver rather than gold to the mint. But the difference between mint ratio and market ratio was so small and intermittent that until early in 1798 there was no movement of silver to the mint. Then the price of silver, even in terms of the now inconvertible Bank of England notes, fell to a figure that made it profitable to bring silver to the mint, but the Privy Council Committee on Coin ordered the Mint to stop coinage. This administrative action was soon ratified by parliament, but without permanently repealing the legal bimetallic standard. At about the same time Lord Liverpool, a member of the Committee on Coin, drafted a memorandum urging the legal de-monetization of silver. The question of the coinage of silver soon ceased to be of immediate practical importance, for in 1799 the London price of silver went above the coinage price; and as the war continued the depreciation of the pound in the foreign exchanges was a much more pressing problem than the question of whether, at some undetermined date in the future, silver could be freely coined. Liverpool's memorandum was published only in 1805,[16] and aroused virtually no public discussion at the time, when other financial problems seemed much more important to a practical-minded people than the theoretical aspects of a future contingency. What discussion may have gone on in informal meetings of Treasury officials and the Bank of England one does not know, but so far as the record shows no one in official circles gave any thought to the problem, one way or the other. The change in the relation of silver to gold had been within a 5 per cent range for around a century, and the consequences of choosing one of the metals over the other had none of the practical consequences of the great fluctuations in the gold-silver ratio after 1873. Ricardo had discussed, without much conviction one way or the other, the relative merits of the two metals as a standard, at one time showing a preference for silver, and later for gold.[17]

15   Sir John Craig, *The Mint: A History of the London Mint from* A.D. *287 to 1948* (Cambridge: Cambridge University Press, 1953) gives statistics on the coinage of gold and silver, pp. 417-19.

16   *A Treatise on the Coins of the Realm* (Oxford and London: 1805).

17 For a fuller discussion on this point see R. S. Sayers, 'Ricardo's Views on Monetary Questions' *Quarterly Journal of Economics,* LXVII, February 1953, pp. 36-37.

In 1816 legislation provided for a single gold standard, not, so far as available evidence indicates, because of any reasoned preference for gold over silver as a standard of value, but in order to make it possible to have silver coins that would remain in circulation. With the market price of silver well above the coinage price, the small coin situation had become even worse than before 1797. The experiment of stamping Spanish silver coins with the head of George III to pass current as equal to a specified amount of British money had not been satisfactory.[18] Accordingly the Lords of the Committee of Council, without holding public hearings, recommended[19] the adoption of a single gold standard, with fiduciary silver coins to be legal tender up to only £2. Despite opposition in the Lords from the Earl of Lauderdale and in the Commons by Alexander Baring, legislation was passed that meant that when the Bank of England resumed cash payments, it would be on the basis of a single gold standard. With the hindsight of history, it is amazing that a decision of such importance for England, and by England's example for the entire world, should have been made without benefit of full analysis, and largely on the basis of details of small coin convenience, and not on larger issues of economic policy. Thus was formally established the gold standard which became effective with the resumption of cash payments in 1821 and survived for 93 years.

In the next 30 years there was a continual attack, both in and out of parliament, on the resumption of cash payments of 1821. In parliamentary papers the problem came up only peripherally, usually in connection with committees on banking, and parliament voted down by large majorities several proposals to investigate the monetary standard. The attacks took three main forms: (1) the resumption of 1821 should have been with a smaller gold content of the pound; (2) resumption should have been either on the basis of an outright silver standard, or of bimetallism at the legal rate of 1797, which would have meant a pound about 5 per cent less valuable in terms of gold, assuming that the action did not change the market ratio of the two metals; and (3) inconvertible paper money should have been continued. The first issue was not, strictly speaking, over what the standard should be, but over the current value at which the pound should be stabilized, regardless of the standard. The third issue was rarely presented in pure form, but associated with criticism of the rate of

18   For an account of the stamped silver, see Maberly Phillips, *The Token Money of the Bank of England, 1797 to 1816* (London: 1900). A fuller discussion of the legal demonetization of silver in 1816 is in my *Development of British Monetary Orthodoxy*, pp. 64-67.

19 *Report of the Lords of the Committee of Council, appointed to take into Consideration the State of the Coins of this Kingdom*, Sess. 1816 (411), vol. 6, p. 402. This is not in the IUP series.

stabilization of 1821, or with proposals for a silver standard or bimetallism. The closest approach to a consistent support of inconvertible paper came between 1816 and 1847 from a Birmingham group, of which Thomas Attwood was the most articulate spokesman.[20] However, the most continuous and consistent attack on the Act of 1821 came from supporters of the silver standard or bimetallism. Some of the leading spokesmen for silver were men of conservative political views, for in the England of that day support of silver as a standard had none of the politically radical connotations that it came to have in the United States in the latter decades of the century. In the hearings of 1819 discussion was concentrated on when, and how, the Bank of England should resume cash payments, and no mention was made of the possibility of a silver standard or of bimetallism, except by Alexander Baring in the Commons hearings (12 March 1819, p. 192) and Lords hearings (3 May 1819, p. 104), and by Isaac Lyon Goldsmith in the Lords hearings (23 April 1819, p. 265). The doubts of Baring about a single gold standard continued until his death in 1848, and his hopes for monetizing silver probably came closer to success than history has recognized. As early as 1816, as a member of the Commons, he had spoken favourably of silver as a standard, and at least half a dozen times during his long parliamentary career he expressed the same idea. In evidence in 1836 before the Commons *Select Committee to Inquire into the State of Agriculture* (q. 17.760),[21] Baring again urged a silver standard or bimetallism; and in the 1830s and early 1840s several parliamentary witnesses, and nearly a score of pamphleteers, spoke well of silver or bimetallism.[22]

The closest that the silver supporters came to success was in 1826, 1827 and 1828, as an aftermath of the crisis of December 1825. To Alexander Baring's support was added that of William Huskisson; and in 1828 both Robert Peel, and the Duke of Wellington when Prime Minister, were sympathetic toward Baring's proposal. Baring testified in favour of silver before the Board of Trade, and the Governor and Deputy Governor of the Bank attended the Privy Council to explain the Bank's position, which was not favourable to silver.[23] For reasons that are not clear, neither Baring

20 I have edited, with an Introduction, several of Attwood's pamphlets, representative of his ideas, in *Selected Economic Writings of Thomas Attwood* (London: London School of Economics and Political Science, 1964).

21 IUP Agriculture: 4.

22 For further details of the support for silver or bimetallism, see my *Development of British Monetary Orthodoxy*, pp. 124-26, 164, 181-82.

23 Baring's testimony, the government's questions, and the Bank's answer were printed in 1830 and reprinted in 1848. They are in IUP Monetary Policy: Currency 2, pp. 11-22.

nor the government pressed the issue. However, until the late 1840s, the sporadic support of silver was never strong enough to provoke a head-on collision on policy. Baring, although not making a public issue of the matter, continued in principle a supporter of silver. Professor R. S. Sayers' suggestion[24] that the provision in the Bank Act of 1844 that one-fifth of the Bank's reserves could be kept in silver was due to Baring's influence, is plausible, although there is no direct evidence on the point.

From the close of the Napoleonic wars until 1848 support of silver had been based primarily on the idea that this would give a slightly higher price level than a gold standard. This situation was quickly reversed by the Californian and Australian gold discoveries, and soon fears were expressed that the retention of the gold standard might be as inflationary as the paper money proposals of the Birmingham economists, but no such inflation followed. The 1850s provided voluminous pamphlet and periodical literature,[25] but parliamentary speakers calling for investigation received virtually no support. References to the new gold, in the Commons' committee hearings of 1857 and 1858 on the Bank Acts[26] were largely incidental, with no suggestion that the new supplies of gold called for any change in the monetary standard. The gold standard by the 1860s had become a cornerstone of the British economy, and virtually outside the area of debate.

In the 1870s silver again came into the arena of British economic controversy by the side door of India. India was on a silver standard, but the relatively minor swings in the gold-silver ratio since the dominance there of the British Raj had not presented serious problems. The decline in the gold price of silver, beginning in 1873, with a depreciation of 10 per cent in three years and continuing downward until in the early 1890s the ratio was over 30 : 1, presented a new set of problems—in particular the effect upon the Indian foreign trade, and upon Indian remittances to England. This was investigated by a select committee in 1876, and the following decade produced a series of documents published as parliamentary papers.[27] With the continuance of the decline in the gold price of

24 'The Question of the Standard, 1815-44', *Economic History*, III, February 1935, pp. 100-01.
25 Michel Chevalier's book was translated by Richard Cobden and published under the title *On the Probable Fall in the Value of Gold* (Manchester, London and Edinburgh: 1859), and was widely read. R. S. Sayers, 'The Question of the Standard in theEighteen-Fifties', *Economic History*, II, January 1933, pp. 577-601, reviews the controversy and cites much contemporary literature; I review the controversy in *Development of British Monetary Orthodoxy*, pp. 240-49; Craufurd D. Goodwin, in 'British Economists and Australian Gold', *The Journal of Economic History*, XXX, June 1970, pp. 405-26, treats all aspects of the economic effects of the Australian gold discoveries, but the discussion of the direct monetary results is on pp. 407-11.
26 IUP Monetary Policy: General 8 and 9.
27 IUP Monetary Policy: Currency 6, *Report and Papers Relating to Indian Currency and the Depreciation of Silver, 1876-96*.

silver, the British government, at the request of the government of India, in 1893 appointed a committee under the chairmanship of Lord Herschel. The committee, after taking extensive testimony, recommended the closing of the Indian mints to the free coinage of silver.[28] Later that year the Indian government adopted the recommendation, and after a depreciation of the rupee from 21d. in 1890 to less than 16d. just before the closing of the mints, and to under 13d. in 1894, the rupee was raised to 16d. in 1898 by what was in effect a gold exchange standard. Another Royal commission of 1898—the Fowler Commission—recommended the formal acceptance of a 16d. rate.[29] This was adopted, but the continuing problems of Indian foreign exchange and banking are beyond the period of this commentary.[30]

The decline in the gold price of silver first became an economic problem for Britain by way of India, without any movement for a change in England's gold standard. But beginning in the late 1870s, and increasingly in the 1880s, the complications that fluctuations in the Indian exchange were creating for England, the pressure from the United States for bimetallism, and the domestic economic problems resulting from falling gold prices, led to serious consideration of the possibility of international bimetallism. Britain participated in several international monetary conferences, and in 1887 the government appointed a *Royal Commission on Recent Changes in the Relative Values of the Precious Metals.*[31] A divided commission recommended bimetallism, but the government did not push the proposal, and the movement never got off the ground on the international political level. The outpouring of gold from the Rand soon settled the question of the gold standard for that

28   The Herschel Committee Report, and papers relating to it, are in IUP Monetary Policy: Currency 7, *Reports and Papers Relating to Indian Currency, 1893-99.*
29   The Report of the Fowler Committee, and a part of its Minutes of Evidence are in IUP Monetary Policy: Currency 7, *Reports and Papers Relating to Indian Currency, 1893-99;* the balance of the evidence and papers are in IUP Monetary Policy: Currency 6, *Further Minutes of Evidence Taken by the Committee on Indian Currency with Appendices and Index. 1899.*
30   For a survey of Indian banking and currency up to 1913 see E. W. Kemmerer, *Modern Currency Reforms* (New York: Macmillan, 1916), pp. 1-152, and J. M. Keynes, *Indian Currency and Finance* (London: Macmillan, 1913), reprinted in 1971 as Volume I in *The Collected Writings of John Maynard Keynes* (London: Macmillan, for the Royal Economic Society). The Kemmerer volume has an extended bibliography, including many periodical articles.
31   IUP Monetary Policy: Currency 4, *Reports and Papers Relating to the International Monetary Conference and Changes in the Relative Values of Precious Metals, 1878-87* has the reports of these international conferences and the first report and minutes of evidence of the *Royal Commission on Recent Changes in the Relative Values of the Precious Metals* (1887); IUP Monetary Policy: Currency 5 includes further minutes of evidence and subsequent reports. The final report of the Royal Commission was reprinted in 1936 with an introduction by Ralph Robey as *The Monetary Problem. Gold and Silver* (New York: Columbia University Press).

generation, and it remained firm and unchallenged until the guns of August created a new situation in 1914.

The role of the Bank of England

The Bank of England was established in 1694, but it is anachronistic to consider it in its first century as anything approaching a central bank.[32] It was, in its origin, primarily an agency of Whig war finance; it had no monopoly of the note issue, it did not hold the country's banking reserves. The Bank came gradually to take on the functions of a modern central bank only by a process of trial and error, and not by reading tracts on central banking theory. A small step towards its evolution into a central bank appears to have been unplanned, and so far as the records go unexplained—the voluntary dropping of note issue by the private banks of London, thus giving the Bank the monopoly of the note issue in the London area.[33] But it was not until half a century later, in 1844, that effective steps were taken to give the Bank a monopoly of note issue in all of England. There was no law, or even tradition, that required other banks to hold reserves with the Bank of England. But as a matter of convenience country banks, increasingly after the middle of the eighteenth century, came to keep reserves in the form of deposits with London banks, who in turn held deposits with the Bank. Whatever may have been the situation before the outbreak of war in 1793—and specific information is fragmentary—it soon became clear that the nation's ultimate banking reserves were in the Bank of England's vaults, and that no matter where or how a panic might start, it caused a drain on the Bank's specie. This situation was succinctly stated in the report of the Lords' Committee of Secrecy in 1797:[34]

> The Bank of England is at the Head of all Circulation. It is the great repository of the spare cash of the Nation, and alone carries Bullion to the Mint to be coined. It is subject, on that account, to be called on for Cash, directly or indirectly, by those who are in Want of it, and is necessarily sensible of every failure or distress, which arises from any Deficiency or want of Coin, in every part of this Kingdom or Ireland.

32   For a history of the Bank of England to 1903 see A. Andreades, *History of the Bank of England* (London: P. S. King, 1909; 2d edition, 1924), and Sir John Clapham, *History of the Bank of England,* 2 vol. (Cambridge: University Press, 1945). R. S. Sayers is now writing, with the cooperation of the Bank, its history for the years 1890-1939, which is due to appear in 1974.

33   No writer on the history of English banking has been able to state with assurance just when or why this action was taken; and repeated inquiries from English economists over the past 15 years have failed to clarify the situation.

34   IUP Monetary Policy: General 1, p. 559.

With the gradual, but unplanned extension of fractional reserve banking, the demand liabilities of banks became far in excess of their cash available for satisfying these demands. This posed a problem when there was a change in the public's desire to hold coin as opposed to bank notes—who was to supply the currency to meet the new situation? Was it the responsibility of the Bank of England? The Bank's history is silent on this matter up to 1793. Insofar as the Bank may have expanded credit in panic periods, its action apparently was assimilated with a general policy of taking care of individual customers who were in trouble, and not rationalized in Bagehotian terms of the special responsibilities of a central bank to the money market.

The events of 1793 brought to the surface in a form that could not be avoided this issue of the Bank's responsibility. As indicated earlier the Bank refused to accept the responsibility, the government was not prepared to press the matter and aid came from the government in the form of exchequer bills. After the suspension of cash payments in 1797 Henry Thornton, in testimony before the Commons committee, stated, in words that have the ring of Walter Bagehot over 70 years later, the need for the Bank to extend credit in time of crisis:[35]

I conceive, therefore, that the Bank of England can find no safety for themselves, except by seeking it in the safety of the commercial world, in the general support of Government credit, and of the general prosperity of the Nation. It follows, therefore, that if any great suppression of their Notes is injurious to general credit, it must be injurious also to the Bank of England itself; and that the Bank of England, in respect to the issuing of Notes, does not stand on the same footing as an individual Country Banker.

During the Suspension years and for several years thereafter, the question of the Bank of England's responsibility to take action in time of crisis was overshadowed by controversy over exchange rates and the standard. The Bank's role in time of crisis came up in these years only as a subordinate issue, but the lines of the controversy that was to erupt later in connection with the debate over the note issue provisions of the Bank Act of 1844 and over the Bagehot principle are evident in the differing views of David Ricardo and Henry Thornton. Ricardo, with his mechanistic view of the relation between money supply and prices favoured a circulation virtually tied to the Bank's specie holdings [36] whereas Thornton's view was that the Bank should have a more flexible

35 IUP Monetary Policy: General 1, p. 99.

36 In particular his *Proposals for an Economical and Secure Currency* (1816) and in his posthumous *Plan for the Establishment of a National Bank* (1824).

policy. The Bullion Report, however, took essentially the Thornton view:

> A much smaller amount [of currency] is required in a high state of
> public credit, than when alarms make individuals call in their advances,
> and provide against accidents by hoarding; and in a period of mutual
> commercial security and private confidence, than when mutual distrust
> discourages pecuniary arrangements for any distant time.[37]

But this was not the pressing issue as long as the suspension of cash
payments continued, and in the hearings of 1819 the question of the
Bank's role as a lender of last resort, in contrast with its responsibility to
maintain a convertible currency, received little attention. In 1825 and
1826 the issue again surfaced; in December 1825 the Bank threw in its
resources to relieve the panic; and again in March 1826, under government
pressure, came to the aid of the still distressed money market.[38]

In the situation of late 1825 and early 1826 the Bank of England, albeit
reluctantly and belatedly, had acted much the way Walter Bagehot might
have recommended. But the issue was never squarely faced in any
parliamentary investigation, and within the Bank Court itself there seems
to have been, for the next half century, considerable difference of opinion
as to just what the Bank's responsibilities were. To some degree the
uncertain, and even shifting opinion within the Bank can be explained in
terms of personality. But the explanation goes deeper than that.

The events of 1825 and 1826 had led to a widespread opinion that the
Bank, then subject to no legal reserve requirements of any kind, had
brought on the crisis by its expansive credit policy. No well formulated
proposals emerged, but there began to develop a public opinion which
would be receptive to specific proposals. As early as 1827 James
Pennington prepared a memorandum urging what was the basis of the
Bank Act of 1844—tying fluctuations in the Bank's notes to fluctuations
in its specie reserve.[39] In the hearings of the Commons Committee of
Secrecy on the Bank of England Charter[40] of 1832, the question of the
Bank of England's responsibility, and of restrictions on its credit
expansion, recurred repeatedly, although there was little head-on clash

---

37   IUP Monetary Policy: General 1, p. 212.

38   For a more detailed account of this situation, see Clapham, *The Bank of
England,* II, pp. 98-102, 108-09; Andreades, *History of the Bank of England,*
pp. 248-53; my *Development of British Monetary Orthodoxy,* pp. 111-20. I give
further details of these developments in my 'An Historical Confusion in Bagehot's
Lombard Street', *Economica,* n.s. vol. XXXIV, February 1967, pp. 80-83.

39   An account of Pennington's life, writings and influence, and a reprint of his
principal writings, are in R. S. Sayers, *Economic Writings of James Pennington*
(London: London School of Economics and Political Science, 1963).

40   IUP Monetary Policy: General 4.

over specific proposals. However, two points indicative of what was to come can, at least with the wisdom of hindsight, be seen as emerging out of the hearings. First, the preponderance of opinion that there was need for an institution such as the Bank of England, with a special but not clearly defined position, and possibly with a monopoly of note issue; and secondly, the Bank should have a more conscious and recognized policy of relating its credits to its reserves. John Horsley Palmer explained the Bank's recently adopted policy, that came to be known as the Palmer rule: when the foreign exchanges were on the point of becoming unfavourable, the Bank should hold specie reserves equal to one-third of its notes and deposits, and from that point on notes and deposits should vary directly with specie reserves.[41]

The investigations of joint stock banking in the late 1830s had only incidental reference to Bank of England policy;[42] but the hearings before the Committee of 1840[43] provided a clear-cut issue between Samuel Jones Loyd (later Lord Overstone), who in effect argued for a policy of requiring the Bank's notes to fluctuate with specie holdings, and Thomas Tooke, who wished to leave reserves to the discretion of the Bank. The general position of Loyd is associated with the term 'Currency School'; the position of Tooke with the term 'Banking School'. However, the issues involved were much more complex than is suggested by the capsule summary so often taught to students that the Currency School held that the deposits were not money, that the Banking School held that deposits were money. Such a summary obscures the basic point at issue, which was Rules vs. Discretion.[44]

In the light of the development of central banking Tooke was right in his support of discretion, but in the political setting of the time it was Loyd's anti-discretion view that won the legislative victory. For this there were three main reasons: (1) the increasing strength of free trade sentiment made large sectors of the public look with suspicion at any plan that left discretion to government or to a government monopoly; (2) a widespread belief that the Bank had not heeded the lessons of the panic of

41   For more details on the Palmer rule see my *Development of British Monetary Orthodoxy*, pp. 132-33, 145-46; Elmer Wood, *Englich Theories of Central Banking Control, 1819-58* (Cambridge, Mass.: Harvard University Press, 1939), pp. 102-03.

42   IUP Monetary Policy: Joint Stock Banks 1, *Reports from the Secret Committee on Joint Stock Banks with Minutes of Evidence, Appendices and Indices, 1836-1838*.

43   IUP Monetary Policy: General 5, *Report from the Select Committee on Banks of Issue with Minutes of Evidence, Appendix and Index, 1840*.

44   For a further discussion of this point, see Lord Robbins, *Robert Torrens and the Evolution of Classical Economics* (London: Macmillan, 1958), pp 97-143, and my *Development of British Monetary Orthodoxy*, pp. 187-94.

1825, and that its liberal credit policy, even in the face of declining reserves, had contributed to the near crisis conditions in the money market in late 1838 and 1839; and (3) a feeling within the Bank itself that it would be well, to protect the Bank from public criticism of its actions, to have a legislative limitation on its discretionary action.[45] The legislative result was Peel's Bank Act of 1844, which divided the Bank of England into a Banking Department and an Issue Department. The Banking Department was left free of any reserve requirements; whereas the Issue Department was confined to the issue of notes, which except for £14,000,000 of notes corresponding to the government debt held by the Bank, were to be backed 100 per cent by specie, of which 20 per cent could be silver. Although the law did not so state, the background of controversy out of which the Act emerged gave strong support to the idea that the Bank, in its Banking Department, was to operate on the same basis as any other bank, with no responsibility to the market to act as a lender of last resort. This was essentially a victory for the ideas of Ricardo, who had suggested a State Bank subject to strict regulation of its note issues, and Samuel Jones Loyd, as against the views of Henry Thornton, the Bullion Committee and Thomas Tooke.

Within 22 years England had three panics—1847, 1857 and 1866—that led to the suspension of the Bank Act, that is, permission to the Issue Department to issue additional notes without specie backing. These panics, and in particular that of 1847, stimulated a public debate, both as to whether the rigid reserve requirements against notes should be modified, and as to whether the Bank, regardless of the technical provisions of law, should recognize a public responsibility to support the market in time of crisis. The first two crises were followed by full-scale parliamentary investigations—in 1847 in both the Lords and Commons.[46]

45   The story of the Bank's role in initiating the provisions of the Act of 1844 restricting its right of note issue is given in Clapham, *The Bank of England*, II, pp. 172-81.

46   IUP Monetary Policy: Commercial Distress 1, *First and Second Reports of the Secret Committee on Commercial Distress with Minutes of Evidence, 1847-48;* IUP Monetary Policy: Commercial Distress 2, *Appendix and Index to the First and Second Reports of the Secret Committee on Commercial Distress, 1837-48;* IUP Monetary Policy: Commercial Distress 3, *Report from the Secret Committee of the House of Lords on the Cause of Distress among the Commercial Classes with Minutes of Evidence, Appendix and Index, 1847-1848;* IUP Monetary Policy: Commercial Distress 4, *Report of the Select Committee on the Bank Act of 1844 and the Bank Acts for Scotland and Ireland of 1845 and on the Causes of the Recent Commercial Distress with Minutes of Evidence, 1857-58.* In addition, a committee of 1857, shortly before the panic of that year, examined the operation of the Acts of 1844 and 1845. IUP Monetary Policy: General 7, *Report from the Select Committee on the Bank Acts of 1844 and 1845 with Minutes of Evidence,* Part I, 1857; IUP Monetary Policy: General 8, *Appendix and Index to the Report of the Select Committee on the Bank Acts,* Part II, 1857.

No legislative changes came from these investigations, although the Commons committee of 1847 rejected, by a vote of only 13-11, a statement critical of the reserve requirements of the act of 1844; and the Lords committee of that year held that 'the recent Panic was materially aggravated by the operation of that Statute [Act of 1844]', and recommended amendment of the law. But the Act remained unchanged until 1928. The hearings revealed a divergence of view, both within and outside the Bank management, as to whether the Banking Department was just another big bank or whether it had a responsibility to act as a lender of last resort. No recommendations were made by committees on this point.

The final decision that the Bank had a special responsibility came in an undramatic way in the 1870s, without benefit of a parliamentary committee or of a crisis that called for a clear-cut policy. In practice the Bank of England had been willing to act as a lender of last resort, but its directors had not been willing to state this as a Bank policy. In the spirit of virtually all central bankers in all countries they wanted to keep their options open, and were loath to admit that their actions conformed to any set theory. Walter Bagehot, first in *The Economist,* of which he became editor in 1860, and then in his *Lombard Street* of 1873, drove home the point that in the banking system that history had given England, it was essential that the Bank of England stand as a lender of last resort.[47] No legislation was passed and no resolutions were adopted by the Bank, but from the 1870s on the public believed, and the Bank did nothing to disturb that belief, that in time of crisis the Bank stood ready to come to the aid of the market.

Thus the foundation of the British monetary banking system had been consolidated by 1870: the gold standard; the recognition of the power and obligation of the Bank of England to maintain a stable exchange; and the obligation of the Bank to act as a lender of last resort. Except for the brief consideration in the 1880s of international bimetallism, no parliamentary committee, for the 40 years after 1870, even questioned these foundation stones of policy.

Commercial banks and their note issues

From the perspective of history the other issues were details within this grand strategy of monetary orthodoxy, with one exception—the role of other banks. Until 1826 commercial banks were subject only to the laws applicable to all business, except that no partnership with more than six partners could issue circulating notes. There were no reserve requirements, no restrictions on note issues. Other than the Bank of England, the three

47 For the development of this concept, following the Bank Act of 1844, see Ch. IX, 'The Victory of the Bagehot Principle', in F. W. Fetter, *Development of British Monetary Orthodoxy.*

chartered banks of Scotland, and the Bank of Ireland, there were no joint
stock banks. In England the territorial division between the area of Bank
of England circulation in London and of other banks in the rest of
England (except for Lancashire, where virtually no bank notes circulated)
had developed without planning or conscious policy. In Scotland and
Ireland there was no hard and fast division between the areas of circulation
of notes of private banks and of chartered banks. But the notes of Scottish
banks were not current outside Scotland and the notes of Irish banks not
current outside Ireland. Particularly in the case of the Scottish banks was
local pride a formidable barrier to any moves toward uniform regulation of
banks. No bank notes were legal tender until Bank of England notes were
made so in 1833; although as a practical matter Bank of England notes
were legal tender during the Restriction years, as a result of legal decisions
and technical legislation.[48]

Extensive failures of private note issuing banks took place in 1793, and
throughout the Restriction years bank failures continued, with the
situation particularly bad in 1810, 1811, 1814, 1815 and 1816. From
some quarters, including Ricardo in *Proposals for an Economical and
Secure Currency* in 1816, came the suggestion that country banks be
required to deposit government bonds as security for their note issues. A
similar proposal in a government-sponsored bill in 1818 made no headway,
but following the bank failures of 1825 and 1826 a government measure
was passed forbidding banks in England and Wales to issue notes under £5.
However, the attempt to apply a similar restriction to Scottish and Irish
banks aroused a torrent of protest in Scotland. This protest, in which Sir
Walter Scott was active, was based on an appeal to Scottish nationalism
rather than economic analysis, but it was successful in blocking any
attempt to regulate Scottish banks.[49]

Although little legislative action had resulted in some two decades of
agitation against the note issues of country banks, public opinion was
increasingly that the issues of individual banks were an unstabilizing
influence, and that note issue should be concentrated in the Bank of
England. Peel's forceful leadership on the Act of 1844 sealed the fate of
the English country bank notes, although it was many years before all the
death warrants were carried out. The Act provided that no English country

48   For a fuller discussion on this point, see my 'Legal Tender during the English
and Irish Bank Restrictions', *Journal of Political Economy*, LVIII, June 1949,
pp. 241-53.

49   Parliamentary committees were appointed in both the Commons and the Lords
(IUP Monetary Policy: General 3, *Reports Relating to Banking in Scotland and
Ireland with Minutes of Evidence, 1826-27*), and evidence before them revealed the
strength of the Scottish opposition to any regulation. I discuss this controversy in
Development of British Monetary Orthodoxy, pp. 120-24.

bank of issue was to increase its notes above the amount outstanding in 1844, and no new bank was to issue notes. When a private bank increased the number of its partners beyond six, it was to lose the right of note issue. The Bank of England was permitted to increase its fiduciary issue by two-thirds the amount of these lapsed issues. The process of elimination of these issues was slow, but time took its toll, and the last of these private note issues lapsed in 1921.

The desire of Peel eventually to extend the monopoly of the Bank of England's note issue in Scotland and Ireland foundered, as had the attempt of 1826 to regulate the issues of Scottish and Irish banks, on the spirit of Scottish nationalism. What Peel was able to salvage politically was a restriction, which in practice meant nothing, in an act of 1845, limiting note issue to existing circulation plus holdings of gold and silver coin. Thus Peel established the principle that the government could regulate the issues of Scottish and Irish banks, but those banks in practice remained free to issue notes.[50]

Establishment of joint stock banks

Legislation of 1826 first permitted the establishment of joint stock banks with the right of note issue, but only 65 miles or more from London.[51] At first few were organized, but beginning in 1831 there was a wave of incorporations. In 1833 the Bank Charter Act, in the face of the opposition of the Bank of England, cleared up what had previously been in dispute, that a non-issuing joint stock bank with more than six partners could be established in London; and in 1834 the London and Westminster Bank became the first joint stock bank in London. The Bank of England and the private banks, at odds on most issues, were united in their opposition to these new competitors. Joint stock banks soon became a subject of broader concern, with reports of serious abuses in their operations, and with widespread failures.

There followed the appointment in 1836 of a Select Committee on Joint Stock Banks, and in 1837 and 1838 of similar committees after Victoria's accession to the throne. The evidence of many witnesses, and

50   For a discussion of the note issue situation of Scottish and Irish banks, see my *Development of British Monetary Orthodoxy*, pp. 194-97. The question of note issue in Great Britain and Ireland was investigated by the *Select Committee on Banks of Issue* of 1875 (IUP Monetary Policy: General 9), but after hearing extensive testimony the Committee made no recommendations. This was the last parliamentary investigation of banking before 1914.

51   See S. Evelyn Thomas, *The Rise and Growth of Joint Stock Banking*, I (London: 1934) for a full account of the early history of joint stock banking in England; and also T. E. Gregory, *The Westminster Bank through a Century*, I (London: Oxford University Press, 1936), ch. I-V.

the record of failures, strengthened public feeling that joint stock banks were in need of some regulation, although these committees made no reports. Again in 1840 and 1841 committees investigated banks of issue, and their short reports stressed the need for more information from banks of issue.[52] The immediate legislative effect of these investigations was nil, but they all contributed to the groundswell of opinion that brought about the banking legislation of 1844 and 1845. Except for a law of 1858 making general joint stock company law applicable to joint stock banks, no further substantive legislation on commercial banks, whether private or joint stock, was passed during the century.

Operations of the Mint

Parliament appointed a number of committees that were concerned primarily with technical issues of coinage that would have arisen no matter what the country's overall monetary and banking system.[53] These covered the organization of the Mint; details of its operation; its relations with the Bank of England and with the Company of Moneyers; the trial of the Pyx (testing the quality of coins); and coinage operations for foreign governments. In addition these reports have much information on foreign mints. From the policy standpoint, the most important question in this area was the proposal for an International Coinage System, covered in the Proceedings of the International Monetary Conference, held in Paris in 1867, and the report and minutes of evidence of the Royal Commission on International Coinage. The Royal Commission recommended an international coinage system, but nothing came of the proposal.

Financial institutions and practices

In the first half of the century the interest of parliamentary committees in the monetary and banking field was primarily in basic policy: control of foreign exchanges, the monetary standard, powers and duties of the Bank of England, regulation of the note issue. These issues had been pretty well settled by 1860, and except for the Committee of 1875 on *Banks of Issue* and the Royal commission of 1887 on *Changes in the Relative Values of Precious Metals* were not even touched on by parliamentary committees and

52   All five of these committee reports are reprinted by IUP. The first four were noted on p. 23; the report of 1841 is in IUP Monetary Policy: General 6, *First and Second Reports from the Select Committee on Banks of Issue with Minutes of Evidence, Appendix and Index, 1841.*

53   These are in IUP Monetary Policy: Currency 1, *Report from the Select Committee on the Royal Mint, with Minutes of Evidence, Appendix and Index, 1837;* IUP Monetary Policy: Currency 2, *Reports and Papers Relating to Coinage and the Royal Mint, 1845-64;* IUP Monetary Policy: Currency 3, *Reports Relating to Currency and Coinage, 1866-70.*

Royal commissions. Up to the middle of the century, there were no parliamentary inquiries into the institutional set-up of the monetary and banking system, except for the Bank of England. For this there are two main explanations: (1) until there was general agreement on the broad structure of the system, public controversy was concentrated on what that structure should be; and (2) financial institutions were in the early stages of development, and the problems associated with them, and the abuses that they generated, were limited. Around mid-century, as the broad questions of policy were fading into the background of controversy, problems of the expanding financial institutions—both their abuses and the question of their adequacy to best serve public needs—came more and more to the fore. Apart from the changes in the gold-silver ratio as it affected India parliamentary committees and Royal commissions were primarily concerned, after 1870, in the field of monetary policy with the operations of these institutions. The main topics covered by these investigations were savings banks, foreign lending, the London Stock Exchange and money lenders.

Savings banks

The savings banks developed completely separate from the commercial banking system, as a means of encouraging thrift among workers. In their origin and early history they were far more closely connected with the problems of indigence and poor relief than with monetary policy. As the *Report from the Select Committee on Savings Banks* of 1858 put it:[54] 'Before the year 1817, Savings Banks were merely voluntary organizations, established by some leading gentlemen in their own locality, as a help and inducement to their poorer neighbours to exercise frugality and provident habits . . .' (p. 4). The savings banks issued no circulating notes, and no cheques were drawn on their deposits. Strictly speaking, their operations, at least in their early years, did not raise issues of monetary policy, for they were not creators of money, but dealers in the money created by others. The savings banks appear to have been completely ignored in the great controversies over monetary and banking policy; and they became subject of parliamentary investigation only when they failed. Select committees were appointed in 1848, 1849 and 1857; and then in 1888, 1889 and 1893,[55] and their extensive hearings dealt primarily with problems of management, internal audits to prevent fraud, and investments.

54 IUP Monetary Policy: Savings Banks 2.
55 The reports of these committees, and their minutes of evidence, are in IUP Monetary Policy: Savings Banks 1, 2, 3, 4.

Foreign lending

From Waterloo throughout the century England was an almost continuous foreign investor. In several periods large numbers of bonds went into default, and many equity investments became worthless. This was particularly true of South American bonds in the 1820s; bonds of American states in the 1830s: of the Confederate States and of states of the southern United States in the 1860s; and of bonds and stocks of American railroads and bonds of smaller Latin American countries in the 1870s. Yet with one exception—the Latin American loans of the 1870s[56]—these financial disasters prompted no parliamentary investigations. Why there was this dearth of parliamentary curiosity, which had not been backward about questioning bankers, is something of a mystery, but there are two possible explanations. Up to 1860 the heavy losses on foreign investment were closely associated in time with major controversies over monetary and banking policy, and as parliamentary curiosity is a limited resource, there was simply not enough of it to cover the lower priority problem of foreign investment. Secondly, there was probably a feeling that whereas the monetary standard, note circulation, and Bank of England operations affected the entire country, foreign investment was carried on by individuals in search of profit, and if they showed bad judgement, or failed to remember *caveat emptor,* it was not the responsibility of Parliament, in an atmosphere of *laissez faire,* to save investors from their bad judgement, greed or folly. The evidence before the Committee of 1875 revealed an almost incredible tale of graft in borrowing countries, misrepresentation by London issuing houses, and lack of business judgement by investors; it piques the imagination of the scholar of today to think what would have been turned up had Parliament chosen to investigate the other foreign investment disasters. The committee's report, however, was innocuous, and no legislation followed.

Three years later the *Royal Commission on the London Stock Exchange*[57] heard over 50 witnesses. Although the commission covered a broader field than did the Select Committee of 1875, much of the evidence was on the flotation of foreign loans. It made a number of recommendations, almost all relating to internal regulations of the Stock Exchange. No legislation of importance followed, but as has been the case following similar questionable financial practices in Britain, the force of public opinion, probably aided by behind-the-scenes suggestions and gentle pressures from the Treasury or the Bank of England, did much to improve

56 IUP Monetary Policy: General 10, *Reports from the Select Committee on Loans to Foreign States with Minutes of Evidence, 1875.*

57 IUP Monetary Policy: General 11,

conditions. In any case, never again did British foreign lending produce the excesses of the 1870s.

By the end of the century the foundations of monetary and banking policy had been in place for over three decades, even in foreign lending and the operations of the Stock Exchange self-discipline had removed the most glaring earlier abuses, which had passed outside the orbit of parliamentary investigation. The final investigation of the century, into money lending,[58] was an anticlimax after the historic committees in the earlier years that had probed fundamental issues of monetary and banking policy. Some of the hearings were devoted to the possibility of developing rural credit associations, on the lines of the Raiffeisen societies in Germany; but the larger part of them dealt with smaller consumer loans. The evidence revealed serious abuses in what might be called 'loan shark' operations: high interest rates, and pressure, particularly threats of loss of employment, to force repayment of usurious loans. The evidence, together with the appendices, is a valuable source on the status of small loan operations at the turn of the century. The reports, beyond recommending that courts have authority to review all money lending transactions, had little positive policy to suggest for an effective system of either consumer loans or small agricultural loans.

Decimal coinage

As early as 1816 the suggestion had been made in Parliament for a decimal coinage system, and intermittently for the next 35 years a brochure would mention its desirability. But as long as the standard, the role of the Bank of England, and the regulation of the note issue were unsettled, the internal relations of the money system received scant attention. Not until the Great Exhibition of 1851, which made the British more aware of industrial and technological developments on the Continent, was there a widespread interest in a decimal coinage.[59] In 1852 a *Select Committee on Decimal Coinage,* after hearing extended evidence, submitted a report favourable to decimal coinage.[60] The strength of the movement by then was such that apparently it was no longer a question whether Britain would adopt a decimal coinage, but simply when and what the details should be.

That decimal coinage was not then adopted was due largely to Samuel

---

58   IUP Monetary Policy: General 12, *Reports from Select Committee on Money Lending with Minutes of Evidence, Appendix and Indices, 1897-98.*

59   For a full history of the debate over decimal coinage see Neil Davey, 'The Decimal Coinage Controversy in England', unpublished Ph.D. thesis at the London School of Economics and Political Science, 1957.

60   This is in IUP Monetary Policy: Decimal Coinage 2.

Jones Loyd, who in 1850 had been raised to the peerage as Lord Overstone.[61] Following the report of the select committee, Overstone was appointed to the Royal Commission on Deciamal Coinage,[62] and as a result of his influence the commission, instead of concentrating on how to make work a decimal coinage system that many thought had already been adopted in principle, re-opened the whole question as to whether a decimal system should be adopted. And Overstone, despite the fact that the majority of witnesses favoured the decimal system, succeeded in terminating the work of the commission,[63] after preparing a draft report unfavourable to decimal coinage, which he alone signed. Overstone's effort effectively killed for his generation the movement for a decimal system. It was over a century later that a new movement gave Britain a decimal coinage system in 1971.

61 For details of Overstone's role in the decimal coinage controversy, see the discussion 'Decimal Coinage' in D. P. O'Brien's Introduction in *The Correspondence of Lord Overstone,* I (Cambridge: Cambridge University Press, 1971), pp. 52-59, and the letters and appendices there cited.

62 IUP Monetary Policy: Decimal Coinage 1.

63 IUP Monetary Policy: Decimal Coinage 2, *Final Report of the Royal Commission on Decimal Coinage with Minutes of Evidence, Appendix and Index, 1859-60.*

The Documents

MONETARY POLICY: GENERAL

Britain by the middle of the nineteenth century had become the world's banker and her currency had become the *de facto* international unit of account. This role was made possible because of the relative strength of the British economy and the general stability and responsibility of British financial institutions.

The papers in this set document the evolution of British central banking theory and techniques of credit control from the early report on commercial credit at the start of the French war in 1793 to the important policy reports on money lending issued in 1897 and 1898.

Among the important aspects of monetary policy dealt with was the development of the Bank of England's responsibility as the nation's central regulatory bank and lender of last resort during financial crises. The problem of note issue gave rise to an extended controversy. The directors of the Bank found themselves defending their policy against the leading economists of the day including Thornton, Malthus and Ricardo. This controversy appears in several volumes of this set and particularly in the famous report of 1810 on the *High Price of Gold Bullion*. The controversy was finally resolved, after financial crises in 1825, 1836 and 1839, with the embodiment of the views of the current school in the Bank Charter Act of 1844.

The papers for the latter half of the century reflect the steadily increasing power and experience of British banking institutions. The parliamentary inquiries dealt broadly with the activities of the various Banks of Issue and their relationship to the Bank of England, loans to foreign governments and methods employed in London for underwriting these loans, the origins and objects of the London Stock Exchange and, finally, the state of the law regarding money-lenders, their excessive interest rates and extortionist practices.

Many of the reports contain evidence not only of bank directors and noted economists but also of bank officials who describe the organization and methods of banking during the period.

Monetary Policy: General 1 Reports relating to monetary and banking policy with minutes of evidence, 1793-1811. (584 pp.)

The outbreak of the French War in February 1793 was followed by a financial crisis that led to the appointment of a select committee of the

Commons, which recommended the issue of exchequer bills. Following the suspension of cash payments in 1797 both the Commons and the Lords appointed secret committees. The evidence of Henry Thornton before these committees is notable for his emphasis on the central role of the Bank of England in the country's monetary system. The subsequent depreciation of the pound on the foreign exchanges, due both to expansion of note issues by the Bank of England, and to heavy foreign payments, led to the appointment of the Bullion Committee of 1810, under the chairmanship of Francis Horner. The analysis of the Report on the causes of exchange depreciation and of the actions necessary to maintain a stable exchange, although in the war-setting not accepted by the Government, became the basis for the resumption of cash payments in 1821, and from then until 1914 of the international gold standard.

Original references

1826	(23) III	Commercial credit, Sel. Cttee. Rep. (first printed 1793).
	(26)	Bank of England, Secret Cttee. Reps., mins. of ev., etc. (first printed 1797).
1807	(108) II	Public expenditure, Sel. Cttee. Rep.
1810	(349) III	Price of gold bullion, Sel. Cttee. Rep., mins of ev., etc.
	(17)	Bank of England, Secret Cttee. HL. Rep. (first printed 1797).
1810-11	(52) II	Commercial credit, Sel. Cttee. Rep.

Monetary Policy: General 2 Reports relating to the Bank of England with minutes of evidence, 1819. (804 pp. 2 folding tables)

The advisability of resuming cash payments, is the subject of the committee reports in this volume. Robert Peel was chairman of the commons committee. Witnesses included many leading figures in economics and finance, among them Matthias Attwood, Alexander Baring (later Lord Ashburton), Nathan Rothschild, David Ricardo and Thomas Tooke, and directors of the Bank of England. In the face of strong opposition from Bank of England spokesmen, the committees accepted the basic position of the Bullion Committee of 1810, and their recommendation that cash payments be resumed was approved by Parliament and payments were resumed in 1821.

Original references

1819	(202 & 282) III	Bank of England, Secret Cttee. Rep. mins of ev., etc.
	(326)	Cash payments, resolutions.
	(338)	Cash payments, Bank of England, representation.
	(291)	Bank of England, Secret Cttee. HL. Rep., mins. of ev., etc.

Monetary Policy: General 3   Reports relating to banking in Scotland and Ireland with minutes of evidence, 1826-27. (548 pp. 2 folding tables)

Scottish reaction to an attempt by the government to forbid the issue of notes under £5 denomination led to the appointment of the select committees whose reports are contained in this volume. Both Scottish and Irish banks were dependent on small depositors and small loans because of the agricultural nature of the national economies. Witnesses pointed out that great difficulties might arise in these countries for all sections of the population if the small notes were withdrawn. The commons committee, chaired by Robert Peel, recommended that Scottish banks be allowed to continue to issue notes under £5 in denomination, but favoured the gradual elimination in Ireland of notes under £5.

Original references

1826 (402) III	Promissory Notes in Scotland and Ireland, Sel. Cttee. Rep., mins of ev., etc.
1826-27 (245) VI	Circulation of Promissory Notes in Scotland and Ireland, Sel. Cttee. HL. Rep., mins. of ev., etc.

Monetary Policy: General 4   Report from the secret committee on the renewal of the charter of the Bank of England with minutes of evidence, appendix and index, 1831-32. (684 pp.)

Although the central subject of this report concerns the Bank of England, the evidence provides an extensive review of the entire British banking system of the period. The committee heard evidence from many prominent financiers, including Samuel Jones Loyd and John Horsley Palmer, governor of the Bank of England. Much of the evidence deals with the responsibility and policies of the Bank towards the private and also the joint stock banks.

The evidence made clear the position of the Bank of England as the holder of the nation's gold reserves, and Palmer's explanation of what came to be known as the Palmer rule, by which the Bank's specie reserves were to fluctuate with changes in note and deposit liabilities, was a forerunner of the somewhat different provisions of the Bank Act of 1844. The committee issued no recommendations, but the Bank's charter was renewed.

Original reference

1831-32 (722) VI	Bank of England, Secret Cttee. Rep., mins. of ev., etc.

Monetary Policy: General 5   Report from the select committee on Banks of Issue with minutes of evidence, appendix and index, 1840. (832 pp.)

The problems arising from the Bank of England's responsibility as lender of last resort in time of financial crisis led to the appointment of the select committee on banks of issue whose first report is contained in this volume. The evidence covered the whole field of Bank of England policy, with particular emphasis on its action in times of financial pressure and specie export. The evidence of Samuel Jones Loyd and Thomas Tooke is of special interest as they were the leaders, respectively, of the currency and banking schools of thought on monetary issues. The appendix provides financial returns from British and Irish banks of issue for the six-year period ending March 1840.

Original reference

1840   (602) IV   Banks of issue, Sel. Cttee. Rep., mins. of ev., etc.

Monetary Policy: General 6   First and second reports from the select committee on Banks of Issue with minutes of evidence, appendix and index, 1841. (384 pp.)

The principal problem dealt with in these reports is the desirability of banks of issue presenting frequent statements of their assets and liabilities. Witnesses included bank directors and managers from England, Ireland and Scotland. Details of the mechanics of note issue as well as the methods of banking were given by representatives of private and joint stock banks. The materials in this volume provide an insight into banking practice in the years immediately prior to the passage of the Bank Acts of 1844 and 1845. The appendix contains financial returns relating to banking in the United Kingdom.

Original references

1841   (366) V   Banks of issue, Sel. Cttee. of Secrecy. 1st Rep.
        (410)   Banks of issue, Sel. Cttee. of Secrecy. 2nd Rep., mins
                             of ev., etc.

Monetary Policy: General 7   Report from the select committee on the Bank Acts of 1844 and 1845 with minutes of evidence, Part I, 1857. (544 pp.)

The Bank Acts of 1844 and 1845 had failed to live up to the public's expectation that they would prevent crises, and the committee was appointed to consider if any new legislation was necessary to deal with the problem. John Stuart Mill, one of the witnesses, urged that the Bank of England should act firmly to support credit in times of financial distress. The Bank of England directors were divided on the question of the Bank's role in credit control; several directors felt the Bank's reserves were inadequate for the responsibility. The evidence shows that banking opinion was that the Bank of England should lend freely during crisis periods—a role the Bank was reluctant to assume except to a limited extent.

Original reference

1857   (220) X Pt. I   Bank Act of 1844 and Bank Acts of Scotland and
Sess. 2   Ireland of 1845, Sel. Cttee. Pt. I. Rep., mins. of ev.

Monetary Policy: General 8   Appendix and index to the report of the select committee on the Bank Acts, Part II, 1857. (512 pp. 4 folding tables)

This volume contains the appendix to the report of the *Select Committee on the Bank Acts* and should be used in conjunction with the previous volume. A wide variety of statistical returns are included—currency in circulation, bullion accounts, railway loans, estimates of cost of living increases, and a digest of the evidence presented to the committee.

Original reference

1857   (220-I) X Pt. II   Bank Act of 1844 and Bank Acts of Scotland and
Sess. 2   Ireland of 1845, Sel. Cttee. Pt. II. App., index.

Monetary Policy: General 9   Report of the select committee on Banks of Issue with minutes of evidence, 1875. (584 pp)

This committee was appointed as the result of an attempt by the Clydesdale Bank of Scotland to establish branches in England. The bank had the right to issue notes—a privilege denied to newly-established English banks. As London bankers sought legislation to extend the Bank of England's note-issuing monopoly to Scotland, the committee examined the desirability of a single note issue for the entire United Kingdom. Walter Bagehot, the financial journalist, stated in evidence that while provincial note issues were undesirable their abolition would create more problems than it would solve. The committee made no recommendations, and Scottish and Irish banks retained their right of issue.

Original reference

1875   (351) IX   Banks of issue, Sel. Cttee. Rep., mins. of ev., etc.

Monetary Policy: General 10   Reports from the select committee on loans to foreign states with minutes of evidence, 1875. (744 pp. 1 folding coloured diagram)

The committee dealt with the failure of the Honduran and other Latin American governments to honour their debts to English investors. Evidence was given on the methods used for underwriting foreign loans in London. Witnesses told of loans raised by false pretences and of unscrupulous agents of the borrowing country who frequently created an artificial market in the loans in order to encourage investors to increase their financial involvement.

The committee suggested that more complete information be required in any prospectus for a foreign loan, but was loath to recommend legislative remedies, and 'felt bound to express their conviction that the best security against the recurrence of such evils as they have above described will be found, not so much in legislative enactments as in the enlightenment of the public as to their real nature and origin.'

Original references

1875	(152) XI	Loans to foreign states, Sel. Cttee. Special rep.
	(367)	Loans to foreign states, Sel. Cttee. Rep., mins of ev., etc.

Monetary Policy: General 11   Report of the royal commission on the London Stock Exchange with minutes of evidence, 1878. (440 pp.)

The commission examined the origin, objects, constitution, customs and usage of the London Stock Exchange. Much of the evidence deals with methods of preventing fraudulent dealing, and the abuses in connection with the floating of new company issues and foreign loans. The commission recommended that the Stock Exchange authorities be given greater powers to superintend dealings, that care should be taken in compiling the official list of transactions, that only persons of good repute be admitted to membership and that the Exchange should become an incorporated body.

Original references

1878	[C.2157] XIX	London Stock Exchange, R. Com. Rep.
	[C.2157-I]	London Stock Exchange, R. Com. mins. of ev.

Monetary Policy: General 12   Reports from select committees on money lending with minutes of evidence, appendix and indices, 1897-98. (624 pp.)

This volume contains the reports of two select committees which investigated the practices of money-lenders. The evidence disclosed that the law tended to protect the lender rather than the borrower, and that such laws as did restrict the activities of money-lenders were easily evaded. Some witnesses stressed the lack of credit facilities for agriculture, and urged the formation of cooperative credit associations on the lines of the Raiffeisen societies in Germany. The committee of 1897 simply transmitted the evidence it had received, but the committee of the following year recommended that money-lenders be required to register yearly, to keep books of accounts and to be legally limited as to the amount of interest they could charge, and that the Courts should have the right to upset loan agreements if the borrower was being defrauded.

Original references

| 1897 | (364) XI | Money lending, Sel. Cttee. Rep., mins of ev., etc. |
| 1898 | (260) X | Money lending, Sel. Cttee. Rep., mins of ev., etc. |

MONETARY POLICY: COMMERCIAL DISTRESS

One of the most significant factors in the economic and political life of Britain in the last century was the recurrence almost every 10 years of acute periods of financial crisis and commercial panic. The serious slumps of 1847 and 1857 led to the inquiries published here. The troubles of 1847 resulted largely from a period of heavy speculation in railways, and high imports, particularly of corn. In 1857 depression in United States and other markets sharply arrested an export boom and again plunged Britain into a state of crisis. The classic cycle of inflation and depression can be seen emerging here together with the modern techniques of economic adjustment.

Following the controversial Bank Acts of 1844 and 1845 the Secret Committees of 1848 were divided in their views. The Commons committee supported the Act of 1844 by only a narrow majority, and the Lords committee recommended an amendment of the Act. The committee of 1858 opposed any relaxation of the Act of 1844.

The whole functioning of the banking system and the state of world trade at the time are carefully documented in lengthy appendices and in evidence from representatives of failed country banks and the Bank of England.

Commercial Distress 1   First and second reports of the secret committee on commercial distress with minutes of evidence, 1847-48. (664 pp.)

This committee followed the panic of 1847 and the suspension of the Bank Act of 1844, and included almost all the leading politicians of the period: Benjamin Disraeli, Lord John Russell, Edward Cardwell, Sir Robert Peel, Richard Cobden, Joseph Hume, James Wilson, Sir James Graham and Sir Charles Wood (Chancellor of the Exchequer). The evidence revealed a great diversity of opinion about the Act of 1844, and a sharply divided committee fought over almost all the provisions of its report. The final text recommended no change in the Bank Act of 1844. A second report dealt briefly with Scottish and Irish problems but did not recommend any changes in the banking systems in these countries.

Original references

1847-48 (395) VIII Pt. I	Commercial distress, Secret Cttee. 1st Rep., mins of ev.
(584)	Commercial distress, Secret Cttee. 2nd Rep., mins of ev.

Commercial Distress 2 Appendix and index to the first and second reports of the secret committee on commercial distress, 1847-48. (568 pp.)

This volume contains vital data on the state both of the banking system and of trading at the period. It includes sections on general circulation, the Bank of England, country banks and joint stock banks, stamp duty, rates of exchange, public stocks, railways, canals and docks, and the banks of Scotland and Ireland. In dealing with the recent history of the depression it includes appendices on the number of fiats in bankruptcy and on the importation of cotton from the United States and India. More detailed appendices cover general trade with India, general exports of the United Kingdom and corn imports and exports.

Original references

1847-48 (395, 584) VIII Pt. II Commercial distress, Secret Cttee. App., index etc.

Commercial Distress 3 Report from the secret committee of the House of Lords on the cause of distress among the commercial classes with minutes of evidence, appendix and index, 1847-48. (564 pp.)

The committee investigated the events that led up to the crisis of 1847 and the subsequent suspension of the Bank Act, and also the banking situation in Scotland and Ireland. Among the witnesses were Samuel Jones Loyd, Thomas Tooke, Samuel Gurney, Lord Ashburton, John Horsely Palmer and other directors of the Bank of England, and the Governor of the Bank of Ireland. The committee's long report, generally believed to have been drafted by Lord Monteagle, while insisting that the Bank of England notes should always be convertible, felt that the rigid provisions of the Bank Act of 1844 on note issues had contributed to the crisis, and urged a relaxation of the restrictive clauses of that Act.

Original references

1847-48 (565) VIII Pt. III	Commercial distress, Secret Cttee. HL. Rep., mins. of ev., etc.
(565-II)	Commercial distress, Secret Cttee. HL. index.

Commercial Distress 4 Report of the select committee on the Bank Act of 1844 and on the Bank Acts for Scotland and Ireland of 1845 and on the causes of the recent commercial distress with minutes of evidence, 1857-58. (776 pp.)

The hearing dealt with the events that preceded the panic of 1857 and the suspension of the Bank Act that year; the responsibility of the Bank of England in time of crisis; and the experience of the banks of Scotland and Ireland before and during the crisis. The committee's report supported the Bank Acts of 1844 and 1845, and stressed the strategic role of the Bank of England in time of crisis, but two members offered a minority report critical of the Resumption Act of 1819 and favouring an inconvertible paper money.

Original reference
1857-58 (381) V   Bank Acts and commercial distress, Sel. Cttee. Rep.,
                                   mins. of ev., etc.

MONETARY POLICY: CURRENCY

The 40 papers on currency which comprise this set were originally issued between the years 1837 and 1899 and deal principally with the affairs of the Royal Mint, the vexed international question of bimetallism in the latter half of the century and the Indian silver standard. These papers are particularly valuable for their international scope. They contain detailed information on the activities of mints throughout the world, on international monetary conferences and on the gradual adoption of gold as the dominant metal almost everywhere. The monetary situation in France, Austria, Russia, the United States, India, Japan and Brazil is especially well documented.

The reports on the Royal Mint outline its history and its methods of operation from 'imported ingot to issued money'. Of special interest is a paper of 1845 on the 'trial of the pyx' and a report of 1717 from Isaac Newton, then master of the mint, on gold and silver coin.

The papers on bimetallism contain the views of several famous economists on the working of the gold standard, notably Sir Robert Giffen, Alfred Marshall and R. H. Inglis Palgrave. The fall in the value of silver from 1873 onwards had serious consequences especially in India where the rupee was based on the silver standard and in the United States where new silver mines had been discovered and the price of silver became a heated political issue. Several international conferences on bimetallism were held in Paris but despite pressure from the United States no action was taken to adopt international bimetallism. India retained the silver standard and saw its currency depreciate. Several committees examined the Indian situation towards the end of the century.

Currency 1   Report from the select committee on the Royal Mint with minutes of evidence, appendix and index, 1837. (504 pp. 6 folding tables)

This volume contains a comprehensive account of the history of the Royal Mint and of the mint's operating methods. The evidence and report cover such topics as the relationship of the mint with the Bank of England and the Company of Moneyers, the production of 'private coinage', i.e., coinage undertaken by the mint on behalf of foreign governments, and—for comparative purposes—the working methods of the French mint.

Original reference

1837   (465) XVI   Royal Mint, Sel. Cttee. Rep., mins. of ev., etc.

Currency 2   Reports and papers relating to coinage and the Royal Mint, 1845-64. (440 pp. 1 folding plan)

The principal report contained in this volume deals with the reorganization of the Royal Mint and includes many details of the mint's history and operation. Other papers relate to the conduct of the trial of the pyx and to the relative merits of gold and silver coinage. Of special interest is a short report on the latter subject by Sir Isaac Newton when he was master of the mint.

Original references

1845	(347) XXVIII	Coinage. Pyx jury. Rep.
1847-48	(718) XXXIX	Mint. Mins. of ev. of Lord Ashburton on Cttee. for gold coin, 1828, and Rep. of Isaac Newton on gold and silver coin, 1717.
1849	[1026] XXVIII	Royal Mint, R. Com. Rep., mins. of ev., etc.
1852	(76) XXVIII	Royal Mint. Reps.
1864	(268) LVIII	Weights, measures and coins. International Statistical Congress, Berlin. Rep. of proc.

Currency 3   Reports relating to currency and coinage, 1866-70. (600 pp.)

The International Monetary Conference held in Paris in 1867 recommended the establishment of an international coinage system. This recommendation led to the appointment of a royal commission. Walter Bagehot and W. S. Jevons gave evidence in favour of an international coinage system, and the commission advocated its introduction. Among the reports in this volume is a survey of European currency systems and mints.

Original references

1866	(293) XL	Coinage. H. W. Chisholm, chief clerk of the Exchequer. Rep.
1867-68	[4021] XXVII	International Monetary Conference, Paris, June 1867. Master of the mint and R. Wilson. Rep.
	[4073]	International coinage, R. Com. Rep., mins. of ev., etc.
1868-69	(285) XXXIV	Gold currency. Master of the mint and Col Smith. Rep.
1870	(7) XLI	The Mint Reps.
	(466)	European mints. Deputy master of the mint. Rep.

Currency 4   Reports and papers relating to the international monetary conference and changes in the relative values of precious metals, 1878-87. (744 pp. 2 folding tables)

Bimetallism was a major monetary issue in the 1870s and 80s. The adoption of the gold standard by Germany after the Franco-Prussian War and major silver discoveries in the United States greatly reduced the gold price of silver. Due in large part to the influence of the US government an international conference was held in Paris (1878) to discuss the question. This volume contains the proceedings of the conference and other reports and correspondence relating to Britain's participation. Apart from the US and Italy all the countries represented in Paris were unfavourable toward bimetallism. The 1887 report gives details of the currency systems of foreign countries and the mode of operation of foreign mints.

Original references

1878-79	[C.2196] XXI	International Monetary Conference, Paris, Com. Rep.
1881	(409) LXXV	International Monetary Conference, Paris. Translation
	(449)	International Monetary Conference, Paris. Correspondence between the Foreign Office, the Treasury, the Bank of England and the India Office.
1882	(221) LIII	International Monetary Conference, Paris. Rep. C. W. Fremantle, delegate.
	[C.3229]	International Monetary Conference, Paris. Rep. to Secretary of State for India.
1887	[C.5099] XXII	Recent changes in the relative values of the precious metals, R. Com. 1st Rep., mins. of ev., etc.

Currency 5 Reports of the royal commission on changes in the relative values of precious metals with minutes of evidence, appendices and index, 1888. (728 pp. 1 folding coloured diagram)

The discovery of new silver mines in the United States and the abandonment of silver coinage by Germany and the Latin Union led to a sharp fall in the gold price of silver—a cause of concern to Britain because her Indian empire retained the silver standard. The commission heard evidence from a wide group of bankers, businessmen and economists (including Sir Robert Giffen, Alfred Marshall, J. Shield Nicolson and R. H. Inglis Palgrave). A majority of the commissioners recommended international bimetallism, but a minority report opposed it.

Original references

1888	[C.5248] XLV	Recent changes in the relative values of precious metals, R. Com. 2nd Rep., mins. of ev., etc.
	[C.5512]	Recent changes in the relative values of precious metals, R. Com. Final Rep.
	[C.5512-I]	Recent changes in the relative values of precious metals, R. Com. Final Rep., mins. of ev., etc.

Currency 6 Report and papers relating to Indian currency and the depreciation of silver, 1876-86. (784 pp. 3 folding tables)

The report in this volume deals mainly with the effects of the fall in the price of silver on Indian currency which, like that of most eastern countries, was on the silver standard. The consequent depreciation of the rupee in relation to the pound led to the appointment of a select committee 'to consider the report upon the causes of the depreciation of the price of silver, and the effects of such depreciation upon the exchange between India and England'. The committee gave an extended report on its findings, but made no policy recommendations. The volume also contains papers and correspondence with details on world silver production and use, and on the Indian currency system.

Original references

1876	(338) VIII	Price of silver, effects on the exchange between India and England, Sel. Cttee. Rep., mins. of ev., etc.
1877	(120)LXIII	Price of silver, etc., papers.
	(416)	Price of silver, etc., letter.
1878-79	(208) LV	Price of silver, etc., papers.
	(369)	Price of silver, etc , papers.
1884-85	(227) LVIII	Price of silver, etc., papers.
1886	[C.4868] XLIX	Price of silver, etc., correspondence.

Currency 7   Reports and papers relating to Indian currency, 1893-99. (824 pp.)

The 1893 committee, headed by Lord Herschel, was appointed to consider a request by the Indian authorities that free coinage of silver be stopped as a first step toward the introduction of the gold standard in India. The continuing decline in the price of silver and the depreciation of the rupee in terms of the gold standard currencies adversely affected India's foreign trade and disturbed the domestic economy. The committee recommended that, subject to minor qualifications, the Indian mints be closed to the free coinage of silver, with the idea of eventual adoption of the gold standard.

Original references

1893-94	[C.7060] LXV	Indian currency, Ctte. Rep.
	[C.7060-I]	Indian currency, Cttee., correspondence.
	[C.7060-II]	Indian currency, Cttee., mins. of ev., etc.
	[C.7098]	Indian currency, Cttee. Further papers, etc.
	[C.7086]	Indian currency, Cttee., index.
1898	[C.9037] LXI	Indian currency, Cttee., mins. of ev., Pt. I.
1899	[C.9390] XXXI	Indian currency, Cttee. Rep.

Currency 8   Further minutes of evidence taken by the committee on Indian currency with appendices and index, 1899. (480 pp. 16 coloured diagrams)

This volume contains further evidence on the question of the advisability of India adopting the gold standard. The opposing points of view were put by the economists Alfred Marshall and Sir Robert Giffen. Marshall strongly recommended that India should adopt the gold standard as he felt the entire world was moving towards monometallism and there would be no return to the inherently unstable bimetallic system. Giffen held with the Indian nationalists that, as silver was the traditional coinage, gold would not be readily accepted and any change in the system would cause more problems than it would solve. The appendix contains papers on many aspects of Indian finance and documents dealing with the introduction of the gold standard into Russia, Austrian currency reforms and the currency laws of Japan.

Original references

1899   [C.9222] XXXI   Indian currency, Cttee., mins. of ev., Pt. II.
         [C.9376]   Indian currency, Cttee., apps., etc.
         [C.9421]   Indian currency, Cttee., despatch.

MONETARY POLICY: DECIMAL COINAGE

The Great Exhibition of 1851 increased British interest in the continental system of decimal currency and metric weights and measures. The system was widely favoured in Britain at the time and agitation for its introduction led Parliament to appoint a select committee in 1852 and a royal commission in 1857 to examine the subject. The minutes of evidence and reports of these bodies are contained in the present set.

Decimal Coinage 1 Reports and papers relating to decimal coinage, 1852-58. (784 pp. Diagram of Chinese counting board)

This volume contains the report of the *Select Committee on Decimal Coinage* (1852-53) and the preliminary report (1857) of the royal commission of Lord Monteagle, Lord Overstone, and J. G. Hubbard on the same subject. With one exception, the witnesses appearing before the committee favoured the introduction of decimal currency, and the committee recommended decimalization based on the pound-mil system. The preliminary report of the royal commission simply transmitted the evidence of witnesses and the information collected, which included a description of the decimal and metric systems used in other countries.

Original references

1852-53 (851) XXII	Decimal coinage, Sel. Cttee. Rep., mins. of ev., etc.
1857 [2212] XIX Sess. 2	Decimal coinage R. Com. Preliminary Rep., mins. of ev., etc.
[2213]	Decimal coinage, R. Com. Questions communicated by Lord Overstone.
1857-58 [2297] XXXIII	Decimal coinage, R. Com. Answers.

Decimal Coinage 2 Final report of the royal commission on decimal coinage with minutes of evidence, appendix and index, 1859-60. (376 pp.)

Despite the pro-decimalization views of the majority of witnesses, the royal commission, largely due to the influence of Lord Overstone, rejected the decimal scheme on the grounds that a change in the country's coinage system would cause serious inconveniences to all sections of the community and that the public would not readily accept any new system of coinage.

Original references

1859   [2529] XI   Decimal coinage, R. Com. Final Rep. with draft Rep.
Sess. 2   by Lord Overstone.
1860   [2591] XXX   Decimal coinage, R. Com. App., mins. of ev., etc.

Monetary Policy: Joint Stock Banks (1 volume)   Reports from
   select committees on Joint Stock Banks with minutes of
   evidence, appendices and indices, 1836-38. (1,000 pp. 1
   diagram, 1 folding coloured map)

A secret select committee was appointed to inquire into the operation of
the Bank Charter Act of 1833 which permitted the establishment of joint
stock banks under certain restrictions. The committee's task was to decide
whether it was expedient to make any alteration in the provisions of that
Act. Evidence brought before the committee (1836) established the
necessity of instituting a searching examination into the laws which
regulated joint stock banks. Information provided in the oral evidence and
in the replies to questionnaires covered the capital and shares of many
banks, the number of branches and their situation, the aims of the banks
and the business carried on by them. The report revealed extensive abuse
in the organization and operation of joint stock banks.

   The evidence taken in 1837 strenthened the views expressed in the
1836 report. In addition to expanding the information already acquired it
dealt comprehensively with the banking requirements of the community,
the constitution and operation of the joint stock companies including the
liabilities of shareholders, the issue of legal tender, bills of exchange,
promissory notes, etc., loans and advances to customers, accounting and
types of account allowed, failures and dissolutions of joint stock
companies and the influences exerted by the new banks on the money and
bullion markets. There was also evidence on the Banks of England and
Ireland.

Original references

1836   (591) IX   The establishment of joint stock banks, Sel. Cttee.
                                Rep. mins. of ev.
1837   (531) XIV   The establishment of joint stock banks, Sel. Cttee.
                                Rep., mins. of ev., appendix and index.
1837-38 (626) VII   The establishment of joint stock banks, Sel. Cttee.
                                Rep., mins. of ev., appendix and index.

MONETARY POLICY: SAVINGS BANKS

The great success of the first savings bank founded in an impoverished parish in Scotland by the Rev Henry Duncan in 1810 led to a widespread movement for the establishment of savings banks throughout Britain and Ireland. The increase in prosperity among the lower and middle classes in the latter half of the century provided great impetus to the movement particularly in England where joint stock banks, unlike their Scottish counterparts, did little to encourage small depositors.

Several reports in this set contain accounts of the origin and growth of the savings bank movement and outline the various attempts from 1849 to 1894 to reorganize and update the law in their regard.

The problem of fraud prevention was important throughout the century and several reports deal with this notably the report on the collapse of the Cardiff savings bank in 1888. The account of this bank's origin, growth and ultimate failure is a case study in the difficulties of savings banks.

Other reports deal with the relationship between the banks and the Treasury and with the introduction of official auditing of the banks' accounts which led to the elimination of fraud and the establishment of a reliable and efficient system of trustee savings banks.

Savings Banks 1   Reports relating to Savings Banks and savings with minutes of evidence, 1849-50. (664 pp.)

The failure of Dublin's Cuffe Street savings bank led to the appointment of a select committee to examine the causes of the bank's collapse, and the appointment of a new committee the following year, with practically the same membership. The first committee simply transmitted the minutes of evidence and statistical tables. The report of the second committee dealt in large part with the specific case of the Dublin Bank, but also recommended further legislation for the regulation of savings banks. The report of the committee on the savings of the middle and working classes recommended the amendment of existing law so that small savers could invest more easily in landed property, and legislation to control more effectively workers' partnerships to prevent fraud and violation of the terms of the partnerships.

Original references

1849	(437) XIV	Savings banks, Sel. Cttee. 1st Rep., mins. of ev., etc.
1850	(649) XIX	Savings banks, Sel. Cttee. Rep. mins. of ev., etc.
	(508)	Savings of the middle and working classes, Sel. Cttee. Rep., mins. of ev., etc.

Savings Banks 2 Report from the select committee on Savings Banks with minutes of evidence, appendix and index, 1857-58. (512 pp. 1 folding table)

The increase in working-class prosperity greatly aided the growth of the savings bank movement. Unfortunately many of these banks were dishonestly managed and several serious frauds occurred. This select committee dealt with efforts to reorganize the savings bank movement and to eliminate fraud. The report contains a detailed account of past legislation on the subject together with a description of the operation of the savings bank system. The committee recommended amendment and consolidation of the laws, and placing the management of the general funds of savings banks in a commission of five members.

Original reference

1857-58 (441) XVI   Savings banks, Sel. Cttee. Rep., mins. of ev., etc.

Savings Banks 3 Reports relating to Trustee Savings Banks, 1888-89. (640 pp.)

Despite regulatory legislation, savings banks continued to have problems with fraud and general accounting practice. The first report included in this volume covers a serious fraud at the Cardiff savings bank. The 1888 select committee only transmitted the evidence taken, but the committee was reappointed the following year, and after taking further evidence, the new committee made a number of recommendations on the administration of savings banks, and on the relationship between the banks, the national debt reduction office and the treasury.

Original references

1888	[C.5287] XLIV	Trustee savings banks at Cardiff, Com. Interim rep.
1888	(406) XXIII	Trustee savings banks, Sel. Cttee. Rep., mins. of ev., etc.
1889	(301) XVI	Trustee savings banks, Sel. Cttee. Rep., mins. of ev., etc.

Savings Banks 4 Reports relating to Trustee Savings Banks with minutes of evidence, 1889-94. (432 pp.)

The commission appointed to inquire into the affairs of the failed Macclesfield trustee savings bank heard evidence indicating fraud on the part of employees and laxness on the part of trustees. The commissioners' report reviewed the evidence, and criticized the lack of effective control by the National Debt Commission over the accounts of savings banks. The

volume also contains the report of the commissioners investigating fraud at
the Sudbury savings bank.

Original references

1889	[C.5778] XXXIX	Macclesfield trustee savings bank, Com. Interim rep.
	[C.5778-I]	Macclesfield trustee savings bank, Com. Mins. of ev., etc.
1893-94	[C.6884] LXXXIII	Sudbury, Suffolk. Trustee savings bank, Com. Interim rep., mins. of ev., etc.
	[C.6884-I]	Sudbury, Suffolk. Trustee savings bank, Com. Notes of ev.

Bibliography

For a discussion of the theoretical issues in the monetary and banking controversy between 1797 and 1865, chapters III, IV and V in Jacob Viner's *Studies in the Theory of International Trade* (London: George Allen and Unwin; and New York: Harpers, 1937; reprinted by Augustus M. Kelley, Clifton, N.J., 1965) are still insurpassed. My *Development of British Monetary Orthodoxy* (Cambridge, Mass.: Harvard University Press, 1965) surveys the same period, but with less stress on pure theory and more attention to policy and to the political and social setting out of which policy emerged. Thomas Tooke and William Newmarch, *A History of Prices*, which first appeared in 1838-57 in six volumes, but today is more readily available in reprint editions (New York: Adelphi, 1928; and New York: Johnson Reprint Corporation, 1971), has a mass of material on individual prices. The interpretive comments of the authors, who were adherents of the Currency School, minimize the effect of money upon prices. Sir Theodore Gregory's introduction to the 1928 reprint is an excellent background for the monetary and banking debate between 1793 and 1850. This introduction has been reprinted by the London School of Economics and Political Science (London, 1962). Gregory's *Select Statutes, Documents and Reports Relating to British Banking, 1832-1928*, 2 vols (London: Oxford University Press, 1929; reprinted by Frank Cass, London, 1964 and Augustus M. Kelley, Clifton, N.J., 1964) is devoted in large part to the years before 1880. In addition to many extracts from the parliamentary papers on monetary policy, these volumes have the texts of important legislation and extracts from articles in contemporary periodicals. Gregory's introduction of 60 pages is a discriminating commentary on the issue under debate. Chapters IV and V in Lord Robbins, *Robert Torrens and the Evolution of Classical Economics* (London: Macmillan, 1958), although centered on Torrens' views, are invaluable for an understanding of the monetary and banking issues in controversy in the second quarter of the century. *The Correspondence of Lord Overstone*, edited by D. P. O'Brien, 3 vols (Cambridge: Cambridge University Press, 1971), has much on monetary and banking policy, and part of O'Brien's introduction in vol. I is on 'Monetary Thought' (pp. 70-144).

Sir Albert Feaveryear, *The Pound Sterling*, 2d ed. revised by E. Victor Morgan (Oxford: Clarendon Press, 1963), in chapters 8-11 reviews monetary and banking policy between 1793 and 1866. For a discussion of the debate over the exchange rate between Ireland and England during the Restriction period, and for the Report of the Committee of 1804 on the Irish exchange (not reprinted in the IUP series) and selected evidence before that committee, see my *The Irish Pound* (London: George Allen and Unwin; and Evanston, Illinois: Northwestern University Press, 1955). *The Growth and Fluctuation of the British Economy, 1790-1850*, 2 vols, by Arthur D. Gayer, W. W. Rostow and Anna Jacobson Schwartz (London: Clarendon Press, 1953), has statistical data and interpretive material that is a rich supplement, up to 1850, to the IUP Monetary Policy volumes. A microfilm supplement, available from University Microfilms, Ann Arbor, Michigan, has a wealth of statistics from a wide variety of sources and not found elsewhere in so convenient a form.

For a contemporary theoretical discussion of the issues raised in the early years of the Restriction, Henry Thornton's *An Enquiry into the Nature and Effects of the Paper Credit of Great Britain* (London 1802) is a classic. This was reprinted in 1939 (London: George Allen and Unwin) with an Introduction by F. A. v.Hayek, along with Thornton's testimony before the Lords and Commons committees of 1797 and his speech of 1811 on the Bullion Report, and the Hayek reprint was reprinted in 1962 by Frank Cass (London) and Augustus M. Kelley (Clifton, N.J.). *The Works and Correspondence of David Ricardo,* edited by Piero Sraffa, 10 vols (Cambridge: Cambridge University Press, 1951-55) has much on the controversy between 1809 and 1823, in particular vols 3 and 4 (Pamphlets and Papers) and vol. 5 (Speeches and Evidence). Many individual letters in vols 6-9 discuss monetary and banking problems.

R. S. Sayers' article in *Economic History* (A Supplement to the *Economic Journal*), 'The Question of the Standard in the Eighteen Fifties', II, p. 575-611 (January 1933), and 'The Question of the Standard, 1815-44', III, pp. 79-102 (February 1935), review the controversy over the gold standard. In my Introduction to *Selected Economic Writings of Thomas Attwood* (London: London School of Economics and Political Science, 1964), who up to the middle 1840s was the most outspoken critic of the gold standard, I sketch the history and theoretical basis of Attwood's opposition.

A. Andreades, *History of the Bank of England, 1640 to 1903* (London: P. S. King, 1909; 2d ed., 1924, reprinted by Frank Cass, London, 1966, and Augustus M. Kelley, Clifton, N.J., 1966), although written nearly 70 years ago and without access to the Bank's records, is still worth reading. A more detailed account is Sir John Clapham, *The Bank of England,* 2 vols (Cambridge: Cambridge University Press, 1945). Elmer Wood, *English Theories of Central Banking Control, 1819-58* (Cambridge, Mass.: Harvard University Press, 1939), is an outstanding account of the development of Bank of England operations. E. Victor Morgan, *The Theory and Practice of Central Banking, 1797-1913* (Cambridge: Cambridge University Press, 1943; reprinted by Frank Cass, London, and Augustus M. Kelley, Clifton, N.J., 1965), deals almost entirely with the larger policy issues that confronted the Bank of England. Walter Bagehot, *Lombard Street,* that first appeared in 1873 and has been reprinted over 20 times, including French, German and Italian editions, is a lucid presentation of the need for the Bank to stand as a lender of last resort, and also gives a description of the British money market of the early 1870s and some indication of its historical development to that time. W. T. C. King, *History of the London Discount Market* (London, 1936, reprinted by Frank Cass, London, 1972) has much on the development of the money market in the nineteenth century, and of the conditions that led to the suspension of the Bank Act in 1847, 1857 and 1866.

Sir John Clapham, in *The Economic History of Modern Britain,* 3 vols (Cambridge: Cambridge University Press, 1926-38) discusses monetary and banking developments in vol. I, chs VII, XIII, and vol. II, ch. IX. William Smart, *Economic Annals of the Nineteenth Century, 1801-30,* 2 vols (London: Macmillan, 1910-17; reprint by Augustus M. Kelley, Clifton, N.J., 1964) is primarily a review of the parliamentary debates from 1801 to 1830. Vol. I, ch. XIV ('The Report of the Bullion Committee'), ch. XVI ('Debates on the Bullion Committee Report'); vol. II, ch. VII ('The Struggle against Resumption'), ch. XXVI ('The Speculative Mania'), and ch. XXXI ('The End of the One-Pound Note'), provide a useful legislative background for the parliamentary papers. R. C. O. Matthews, *A Study in Trade-Cycle History* (Cambridge: Cambridge University Press, 1954) has much on the economic fluctuations in 1833-42 out of which the monetary and banking controversies arose, and ch. XI deals specifically with money and banking.

For the details of coinage, aside from Feaveryear, already cited, the following are important: Earl of Liverpool, *A Treatise on the Coins of the Realm* (Oxford 1805; and reprinted by the Bank of England, 1880; reprinted from the 1880 edition by Augustus M. Kelley, Clifton, N.J., 1968); Sir John Graig, *The Mint* (Cambridge: Cambridge University Press, 1953), in particular chs XIV-XVIII and XXI-XXIII; and Maberly Phillips, *The Token Money of the Bank of England, 1797-1816* (London, 1900).

Most of the literature on the standard, and on the Bank of England, has some discussion of commercial banking, but more specialized treatment is in S. Evelyn Thomas, *The Rise and Growth of Joint Stock Banking*, I (London, 1934), and Leslie Pressnell, *Country Banking in the Industrial Revolution* (Oxford: Clarendon Press, 1956). Joseph Sykes, *The Amalgamation Movement in English Banking* (London: P. S. King, 1926), has much on the period before 1900. Volume I of Sir Theodore Gregory, *The Westminster Bank through a Century*, 2 vols (London: Oxford University Press, 1936), although centered on one bank, covers the early history of joint stock banking, as does also R. S. Sayers, *Lloyds Bank in the History of English Banking* (Oxford: Clarendon Press, 1957).

A contemporary discussion of the problems raised by the great increase in gold production after the California and Australia discoveries is in Richard Cobden's translation, to which he contributed a brief preface, of Michel Chevalier, *On the Probable Fall in the Value of Gold* (Manchester, London and Edinburgh, 1859). A selection of British writings, both for and against, on bimetallism, *The Bimetallic Controversy* (London: Effingham Wilson, 1886), was edited by Henry H. Gibbs (later Lord Aldenham) and Henry R. Grenfell, both former Governors of the Bank of England, and favourable to bimetallism. Robert Giffen, *The Case against Bimetallism* (London: George Bell and Sons, 1892), is a collection of papers, beginning in 1879, of one of Britain's most articulate critics of bimetallism. Almost all discussion of bimetallism or of silver in the last quarter of the century in some way touched on the Indian currency situation. Chapters I-IV (pp. 3-94) in Part I–'The Indian Currency Reform'–of E. W. Kemmerer, *Modern Currency Reforms* (New York; Macmillan, 1916) cover Indian developments through 1899, and 'A Selected Bibliography', pp. 149-52, lists the principal literature, including a number of contemporary articles, on the Indian monetary controversy.

L. H. Jenks, *The Migration of British Capital to 1875* (New York and London: Knopf, 1927, reprinted by Thomas Nelson, London, and Augustus M. Kelley, Clifton, N.J., 1973), particularly ch. IX–'The Government Loan Business'–has much on the excesses in the floating of foreign loans that led to the Select Committee of 1875 on Loans to

Foreign States and the Royal Commission of 1878 on the London Stock Exchange. The annual reports of the Council of the Corporation of Foreign Bondholders, starting in 1872, give details on individual government loans in default. H. Oliver Horne, *A History of Savings Banks* (London, New York and Toronto: Oxford University Press, 1947), is a good treatment of the subject.

Neil Davey's unpublished Ph.D. thesis of 1957 at the London School of Economics and Political Science, *The Decimal Coinage Controversy in England.* surveys the history of the controversy. D. P. O'Brien's section on Decimal Coinage (vol. I, pp. 52-59) in his Introduction to *The Correspondence of Lord Overstone* well summarizes Overstone's inmportant role in the controversy. The Appendix of the *Preliminary Report of the Decimal Coinage Commissioners* (IUP Monetary Policy: Decimal Coinage 1), pp. 356-65, has an extensive bibliography of the literature.

The Goldsmiths' Library of the University of London and the Kress Library of Business and Economics at Harvard University have the world's greatest collections of literature on the British monetary and banking problems up to 1850. The Kress Library has published a catalogue of its holdings in four volumes, of which vol. 2-4 cover the years 1777-1848; the Goldsmiths' Library in 1970 published a catalogue of its holdings through 1800, and plans a further volume covering the years up to 1850.

NATIONAL FINANCE AND INCOME TAX

Derek Gregory

Contents

NATIONAL FINANCE AND INCOME TAX

59

Commentary

The context

It is not difficult to understand the preoccupation of pre-1800 English economists with taxation as opposed to expenditure, either as an instrument of government revenue, a burden rebelliously borne, or as a spur or a discouragement to industry and trade. In a period when the macro-economic views of writers such as Smith and Malthus hardly suggested more than a vaguely formed view of 'national income' (though a more possitive idea of 'national wealth'), 'national finance' meant little more to the ordinary man than the capacity of and necessity for the central government to raise revenue by taxation or by borrowing. The objects of central government expenditure were even better recognized and largely a matter of common assumption. To a modern citizen, his 'budget' may simply mean a list of expenditures he has to make in a certain period. At national level the budget emphasizes various financial proposals to meet given expenditures. Indeed, a 'financial budget' which gives tax reliefs and imposes tax burdens often assumes a 'balance sheet' aspect in which true expenditure actually plays no part. In these concepts historical tradition still lingers on even in the more modern term 'public finance'.

The question of the national debt was paramount in the eighteenth century mind and the results of sporadic military ventures in that century had raised the debt from about £20 millions to nearly £250 millions by the beginning of the Napoleonic wars. Nearly half of government expenditure supplied the national debt charge and nearly a third of the remainder paid for the needs of the army and navy.[1] The great areas of future economic and social expenditures were supplied by local government, the church, and private organizations, but, however simply the practical needs of expenditure might be focussed, there was no lack of discussion of the 'proper' functions of the state beyond the necessity to contain a debtor's balance sheet and to provide for current defence.

Recent research has emphasized unorthodox views on government expenditure amongst economists of the 'classical' school and there is

1   Jindrich Veverka, 'The Growth of Government Expenditure in the United Kingdom since 1790', *Scottish Journal of Political Economy,* X, no. 1 (1963), pp. 111-27. In this period of course the national debt and interest and charges on it may be considered as 'war-related' expenditure (see Alan T. Peacock and Jack Wiseman, *The Growth of Public Expenditure in the United Kingdom* in *University of York Studies in Economics, No. 1* (London: Allen and Unwin, 2nd ed. 1967, pp. 52-61). A proportion of 'defence' expenditure came through other channels, e.g. the East India Company absorbed the costs of para-military bases abroad.

revealed a clear pressure for extra-traditional expenditure.[2] Occasionally
the language of some writers erupts into startling echoes of later thought.
Sir James Steuart, perhaps the first economist to use the phrase
'propensity to consume', wrote in 1767 that 'taxes promote industry; not
in consequence of their being raised upon individuals, but in consequence
of their being expended by the state; that is, by increasing demand and
circulation.'[3] Similarly, Petty, a hundred years before, expressed a
government expenditure policy for unemployment and thought it 'no
matter if it be employed to build a useless pyramid on Salisbury Plain . . .
for at worst this would keep their minds to discipline and obedience, and
their bodies to a patience of more profitable labours when need shall
require it.'[4] Again, economic expediency parried the questionable
morality of government expenditure.

Radicals, amongst whom Paine must be accounted the prophet of
modern welfare government expenditure, looked further than the classical
position of allowing expenditure on 'collective' goods or, at most,
providing a simplified public works infrastructure. Paine's proposals linked
taxation with expenditure when he demanded tax relief for the low
incomes, child allowances for every child, old age pensions at 50 years of
age, free education, marriage, birth and death grants, and progressive
taxation throughout the whole range of incomes with total confiscation
over a certain level.[5] Paine supplied the arithmetic for his suggestions and,
far from being an extreme libertarian crank, was one of the most admired
men of his day amongst the powerless populaces in Europe and England.
This was clearly in the spirit of a much later trend which has been noted
by a modern writer: 'The changes in the structure of public expenditure
has been accompanied by a change in its character. The primary purpose
of government expenditure, the satisfaction of wants that are not only
collective by nature, but can only be collectively supplied . . . has declined
relatively to the satisfaction of individual wants.'[6] Paine had of course, the

---

2   Only two of the best known works dealing with this topic are cited here, they
are: Lionel Robbins, *The Theory of Economic Policy in English Classical Political
Economy* (London: Macmillan, 1952), and Bernard A. Corry, *Money, Saving and
Investment in English Economics, 1800-50* (London: Macmillan, 1962), pp. 154-73.

3   Sir James Steuart, *An Inquiry into the Principles of Political Oeconomy*
(London: Millar and Cadell, 1767) ed. Andrew S. Skinner (Edinburgh and London:
Oliver and Boyd, 1966) II, p. 725.

4   Ed. Charles Henry Hull, *The Economic Writings of Sir William Petty*, I
(Cambridge: Cambridge University Press, 1899), p. 31.

5   Thomas Paine, *Rights of Man*, ed. H. Bradlaugh Bonner (London: Watts, 1937),
pp. 219-38.

6   Ursula K. Hicks, *British Public Finances, their Structure and Development,
1880-1952* (London: Home University Library, 1954) p. 18.

example of the poor law relief to satisfy 'individual' wants, but that was an expenditure made by local authorities unsubsidized by the central government in England until the 1870s; furthermore it was not dictated by equity considerations but by crisis situations, bordering at times on insurrection.

Although neither the local nor the central scenes of government were innocent of nascent probings into fields of activity which were in the future, the history of public finance records heavy emphasis on the incidence and justice of taxation. The classical economists gave their main attention to the deleterious effects of tax incidence in an economy which though basically agricultural had powerful undercurrents of commercial, industrial and trading interests. It was inevitable that such considerations should occupy half of Ricardo's inquiry into the *Principles of Political Economy and Taxation* and that Ricardo should see the future of economic science as a distributive problem. With pre-war expenditures almost fixed in headings, if not in amounts, the main direction of thought was for economy in its management. The close identification of management with controllable expenditure took on aggressive form in Burke's address on 'Economical Reform' and official permanence in Pitt's Consolidated Fund Act of 1787. These were but preludes to the retrenchment campaigns of the nineteenth century which achieved their peak in Gladstone's administrative reforms of the 1860s and in the rearguard battle to engineer low, balanced, budgets at the expense of rapidly rising local expenditures.

The claims of tax equity were an inheritance of legal and ecclesiastical forms mixed with philosophic explanations of the harmony of duties and rights owed by the state and its citizens. The broad tax principles which evolved assumed practical shape, though with some paradoxical elements, in the pre-Napoleonic array of fiscal experiments. First, there was the implicit duty of all to contribute to a common necessary fund (i.e. external defence and the inherited debts of the state). Secondly, it was admitted that over and above this, the individual had a basic right in normal times to decide the particular direction his tax contributions should take, via his preferred expenditure pattern. The principle of 'voluntaryism' in taxation was workable in a situation where over 70 per cent of taxes were derived from customs and excise, and where the structure of expenditure on goods and services invited neater divisions into 'necessary' and 'luxury' items of consumption. In addition, it was recognized by the vocal and the powerful, that capital was a particularly dangerous object of taxation. An aversion to taxing the capital of trade and industry was, of course easily derived from mercantilist writers such as Mun and Robarts who were in no doubt that state's intrusion into these activities should even take the 'negative' form of giving bounties and privileges. The word 'capital' could be so variously transformed in a more sophisticated analysis to include circulating and fixed capital and the web of tax incidence could be easily stretched to involve depletion of factor rewards as well as exactions on real capital assets, and to the savings which supplied each. The analysis of this process was the work of Ricardo.

Much of this earlier framework was destroyed by the immense upheaval of the Napoleonic wars. The national debt incurred during the wars was to exceed anything contracted during the many British wars of the next century. Its post-war total was to provoke more furious protests against its 'eating of the national capital' and the burden which it laid on taxpayers, than the comparatively harmonious gavotte of eighteenth century pamphleteers who wished to pay off the debt by a succession of ingenious schemes. The expense of the war induced new lines of thought on common contributions to defence, which had been fairly simple when contributions were light and when individual fortunes made from wars were of forgettable amplitude. The spirit of 'voluntary' taxation was no longer to be tolerated in wartime. In 1797 ideas of taxing capital and income were discussed and rejected in favour of a 'triple assessment' allied with a 'voluntary contribution'. The triple assessment (i.e. three times the amount of the previous year's 'assessed' taxes on expenditure) of 1798 failed owing to frauds and evasions, but 'There was hardly a spot on the globe in which a British subject was resident from whence there were not remittances' for the voluntary contribution.[7] In place of 'voluntaryism' came the income tax in 1799, but the discretion of the taxpayer was not quite dead. In the effort to retain secrecy tax returns were made so bare that the tax remained almost voluntary, and this too, failed. Voluntary taxing was part of a misplaced faith under the new conditions and in Addington's revised income tax of 1803 income was taxed at source to preserve secrecy. This too, eventually fell victim to the requirements of administration and revenue.

Although the eighteenth century tradition of 'voluntaryism' in taxation was broken by the introduction of the income tax (if we except the declining revenue of the land tax) and much later by the reform of the death duties, government revenue was still inevitably at the mercy of consumer, income receiver, or private lender, and, one might add, of a weak and inefficient revenue staff. It is in the nature of expenditure that control is much closer to management and more susceptible to manipulative techniques, though the pressure to avoid control is concentrated in organized departments. It was the task of the government, particularly in

---

7   George Rose, *A Brief Examination into the Increase of the Revenue, Commerce, and Navigation, of Great Britain* (London: Hatchard, 1806), p. 32.

the second and third quarters of the nineteenth century, to evolve methods of purging vested interests in its administrators and its executive officials. To achieve this it had to devise qualitatively different rules which would effectively control an altered bureaucracy in which many larger departments of spending had replaced a few small ones and in which departmental individualism could no longer be tolerated.

The character of public financial history has been summarized in Schumpeter's comment that 'Nothing shows so clearly the character of a society and of a civilization as does the fiscal policy that its public sector adopts.'[8] Where the 'national interest' lay at different times in our history can be traced through mercantilist theories of the 'true' principles of expenditure and taxation, through the free trade pressures of the mid-century, to the welfare budgets of today. But concepts of the national interest lie in the minds and active prescriptions of power groups in society, and are changed only by countervailing forces. The rise of industrial capitalism and democratic voting, were two such typical forces in the nineteenth century, and within the parliamentary papers also is present a constant reminder of the power of Treasury officials as a shaping tool for any programme of reform.

Indirect and direct taxation

So impressive did the famous 1840 *Report on the Import Duties* appear in the early 1840s that it was reprinted in 1841 and 1842. At the height of the agitation for free trade this committee, led by Joseph Hume, produced a concise set of arguments and statistics to prove that the economic development of the nation required the dismantling of the remains of tariff protection. In the biased document which was produced, the overbalanced representation and the witnesses called were aided by the staff of the Board of Trade subscribed to an overwhelming case which for long afterwards was regarded as the official evidence for the strangulation of economic growth.[9] The catalogue of demerits for protection stretched to considerable length, taking in everything from increased smuggling, collection expenses, and food prices, to adverse effects on adulteration, poor rates, and the emigration of skilled workmen and capital.[10]

8 Joseph A. Schumpeter, *History of Economic Analysis* (London: Allen and Unwin, 1954) p. 769.
9 The part played by officials of the Board of Trade is described in Lucy Brown, *The Board of Trade and the Free Trade Question, 1830-42* (Oxford: Clarendon Press, 1958).
10 A convenient resumé of the arguments of the free trade lobby, amongst a vast literature, is that of William D. Grampp, *The Manchester School of Economics* (Stanford: Stanford University Press, 1960), and an even more recent study, that of Norman McCord, *The Anti-Corn Law League, 1838-46* (London: Allen and Unwin, 1958).

Witnesses were not short of the support of economists or lacking in examples from history. The Colbertian regime in France and the Ricardian comparative cost theory were harnessed to prove the case, as was the central theme of the 'wages fund' doctrine that the wages of labour are determined by the abundance or scarcity of employment',[11] the supply factor being an inconvenient one for the free trade argument. Trade relations were an integral part of the report. McGregor, who had had much previous contact with officials of the Zollverein (established in 1835), insisted that the repeal of corn duties, as part of the price of good relations with the Germanic Union, would encourage the Union to control continental smuggling routes as well as helping the continued existence of good markets for British textiles.[12] J. D. Hume also stressed continental connections with his prescient warning of the evils of protection that 'those countries (Germany and continental nations) will some day drive us out of the foreign market'.[13] The imperialistic motive, given colour by Palmerston's remark that it was the 'business of government to open and secure the roads for the merchant', placed the emphasis on 'trade following the flag'.[14]

The efforts of many research workers in the history of trade have been focussed on the untrustworthiness of official statistics in similar publications to the 1840 report.[15] Imports, for example, were affected by changes from 'official' to 'computed' values in 1854, and before this, exports were revised from 'official' to 'declared' values. After the failure of Gladstone's scheme for compiling overseas trade statistics in 1860[16] a further revision of the system of obtaining trade figures in value terms was

11   *Report of the Select Committee in Import Duties,* 1840 (601) V, Mins. of ev. q. 1020 (IUP National Finance: General 1).

12   See Nancy M. Gordon, 'Britain and the Zollverein Iron Duties, 1842-45', *Economic History Review,* XXII, no. 1 (1969) pp. 75-87, also L. Brown, *The Board of Trade* (1958) chapter 6.

13   *Report of the Select Committee on Import Duties,* Mins. of ev. qq. 1384-93 (IUP National Finance: General 1).

14   How far free trade arguments were a cloak for the extension of British world interests and the creation of empire, has been discussed in several studies, for example: J. Gallagher and R. Robinson, 'The Imperialism of Free Trade', *Economic History Review,* VI, no. 1 (1953), pp. 1-15; Oliver MacDonagh, 'The Anti-Imperialism of Free Trade', *Economic History Review,* XIV, no. 3 (1962), pp. 489-501; D. C. M. Platt, 'The Imperialism of Free Trade: Some Reservations', *Economic History Review,* XXI, no. 2 (1968), pp. 296-306.

15   For example, generally, Elizabeth Boody Schumpeter, *English Overseas Trade Statistics, 1697-1808* (Oxford: Oxford University Press, 1960) and Albert H. Imlah, *Economic Elements in the Pax Britannica* (Cambridge, Mass.: Harvard University Press, 1958).

16   *Report of the Select Committee on Charges on Foreign Trade (Customs Act, 1860),* 1862 (429) XII, iii-iv (IUP National Finance: General 4, pp. 555-6).

made in 1870. Reliable trade figures must be counted as a casualty of free trade and the reconstruction of meaningful statistics is a special task of the fiscal historian. It is mentioned here as a caveat against accepting the figures (other than as indicators of volume), no less than the arguments in this particular report, with anything approaching unquestioning faith. The 1840 report is accompanied by the *First Report of the Revenue Commissioners of 1842* which suggested changes in customs organization in Liverpool, the second largest port in the kingdom. The report provides a useful, if short, micro-view at an instant in time.

Although the final collapse of the free trade policy did not come until 1932, in several senses the year 1898 may be taken as a turning point in the movement to restore protection and a critical year for revisionary thinking on public finance. In Europe and the United States, political and economic changes had found their expression in 'economic nationalism'. The McKinley tariff of 1891 and the Dingley tariff of 1897 had their counterparts in Europe when France doubled her export bounties in 1896 and Germany followed suit in 1897. Pressure from the industrial sectors encouraged states to protect and foster developing technologies as the unlimited prospects of growth previously accorded to free trade seemed to be fading. The tariff rivalry of manufacturing nations had a heavy strategical bias in that new technologies were being developed in the armaments industries, and emergent industrial economies were anxious to secure control over raw material supplies in primary producing countries. Such fiscal revisionism, gaining some theoretical support from economists such as List in Germany,[17] clearly invited retaliatory action. The need for state revenue was also part of protectionist pressure, not only to render the 'nation state' solvent and free from the debt of past wars, but also to build its future defence resources and provide funds for social welfare schemes. The 'fair trade' movement in Britain included most of these elements and, additionally, in spite of Harcourt's revised estate duty of 1894, it was felt that the tax base should be broadened—a task of some difficulty if free trade was to be retained.

In the decade before this report (1898 [C.8706] LXXXV) was published the fair trade movement in Britain had had its representatives in such bodies as the National Fair Trade League[18] and later in the United

17   Friedrick List had produced his *Das nationale System der politischen Ökonomie* in 1840, at the crisis of the free trade conflict in England, and this theoretical defence of a tariff system was a widely quoted text to support later German protectionist moves.

18   Sir Thomas Henry Farrer, *Free Trade versus Fair Trade* (London: Cassell, 1882) gives a contemporary summary of the 'fair trade' arguments, but for a more recent example, and an excellent account, see Benjamin H. Brown, *The Tariff Reform Movement in Great Britain, 1881-95* (New York: Columbia University Press, 1943).

Empire Trade League, but straightforward protectionism had been rejected by the early 1890s. It was in 1898 that Chamberlain adopted the idea of a British Zollverein in which the territories of the Empire were to take part in a system of the German plan.[19] The scheme of Imperial Preference obviously meant the end of free trade however, and the scheme was rejected by the Liberal and Labour parties. Even with favourable terms of trade,[20] mass consumption of imported cheap food and the reality of the 'free breakfast table' were sufficient to defer any substantial move to destroy the system which had been perfected in 1860. This opinion was to prove its solidarity again against even more determined reformist moves after the South African war.[21]

Apart from Pittar's short report, the main body of the 1898 report is concerned with a detailed factual listing of valuable statistical and reference material the like of which is not available elsewhere. It can therefore claim to be a most comprehensive reference work of its kind dealing with visible trade. The notes, relevant statutes, records of prohibitions, etc. are useful raw data for the research worker, whilst the rates of duty and quantities involved (as in the 1840 report) have formed part of the raw material for many statistical historians.

In the selection of papers on the income tax are the two examples of parliamentary enquiry into the tax in the nineteenth century. After a break of 26 years, Peel had reintroduced the income tax in 1842 in a similar spirit to Parnell's proposal of 1832, i.e. as a makeweight for revenue lost in reductions and repeals in indirect taxation.[22] The tax, considered as a temporary levy had been renewed before 1851 for terms of several years but, with national finances flourishing at the mid-century, a

19   See Sir Robert Giffen, 'The Dream of a British Zollverein', in *Economic Inquiries and Studies,* II (London: Bell, 1904), pp. 387-404. This essay was originally printed in 1902 and Giffen, who supported free trade, was in favour of closer political ties within the empire but not preferential tariff advantage.

20   For the terms of trade, see W. W. Rostow, 'The Terms of Trade in Theory and Practice', *Economic History Review,* III, no. 1 (1950), pp. 1-20 and, by the same author, 'The Historical Analysis of the Terms of Trade', *Economic History Review,* IV, no. 1 (1951), pp. 53-79.

21   Chamberlain, and his part in tariff reform over the decade 1895-1905, are commented on in Elie Halevy, *Imperialism and the Rise of Labour (1895-1905),* V, in *A History of the English People in the Nineteenth Century* (London: Benn, 1961), also A. W. Coats, 'Political Economy and the Tariff Reform Campaign of 1903', *Journal of Law and Economics,* II (1968), pp. 181-229.

22   Sir Henry B. Parnell, *On Financial Reform* (London: Murray, 1830), perhaps the most influential document of this movement. See also, Benjamin Sayer, *An Attempt to shew the Justice and Expediency of Substituting an Income or Property Tax for the Present Taxes . . .* (London: Hatchard, 1833) for a major contribution to the debate at this time.

section of parliamentarians led by Hume urged that the tax be renewed for one year only and an enquiry be set up to investigate the tax on equity grounds with a possible view to reform. If the movement towards freer trade was to be pursued even more vigorously it was clear to many that the income tax could not retain its temporary guise for long. This intimate connection of the tax with the anti-protectionist faction led reformers like Jeffrey of the Liverpool Financial Reform Association to advocate a permanent income tax as the 'sole source of supplying the public fisc'.[23] In 1851 the excise duty on bricks was repealed (thus was lost another valuable series of statistics for the economic historian), the obnoxious window tax was repealed and other taxes were lightened. In addition, the belligerency of France was feared and the state of national defence was being called in question. Consequently, in view of reduced government revenue and increased expenditure, it was against the background of possible 'permanency' that the reports of 1851, 1852, and 1861 were initiated.

These reports also offer contemporary comment on the administration of the income tax which was giving cause for alarm. Evidence of low morale amongst tax officials was claimed in the Hume report where it was stated that the tax would be operated much more efficiently if it were a permanent charge.[24] Addington's scheme of 1803 whereby tax was deducted at source, had raised large numbers of repayment orders particularly on Schedule A and, in turn, in a situation of almost permanent under-staffing, this work load engendered great freedom for the evasion of Schedule D which became, in effect, a 'tax on conscience'.[25]

---

23 *Report from the Select Committee on Income and Property Tax,* 1852 (510) IX, Mins of ev. q. 5744 (IUP National Finance: Income Tax 1). Also *Liverpool Financial Reform Association Tracts* nos 22 and 23 (Liverpool, 1850) and reprint of the prize essay submitted to the National Confederation of Liverpool, by 'X and Y', entitled *Elements of Taxation* (London: Simpkin, Marshall, 1852). The essay was submitted originally in early 1849.

24 *Report from the Select Committee on Income and Property Tax,* 1851 (563) X, Mins of ev. qq. 2633-4 and 2640 (IUP National Finance: Income Tax 1).

25 Ibid. q. 1471. In the case of Schedule D, it was stated that only 11 falsified returns were discovered and proceedings taken during the period 1842 to 1851 (ibid. qq. 453-4). The pressure towards evasion was great because total exemption was granted only when total incomes were below £150 (established by Peel in 1842 and reduced to £100 in 1853 by Gladstone). In addition, it was extremely difficult to identify aggregate incomes. If, therefore, a taxpayer had an income only slightly above £150 he was immediately liable for the *whole* of the tax on his total income (i.e. on £150 plus the surplus over that figure). Nevertheless some witnesses, against the evidence afforded by taxpayer frequency distribution tables, denied that the exemption system was mainly responsible for evasion (see ibid. qq. 2408, 2649, 2736 and 3240).

Neither of the inquiries were sponsored or supported by the government, nor did they lead for many years to revised legislation.[26] For the historian, the statistics contained in the reports are to be treated with caution, especially if they are to be taken as indicators of national income growth, or as measures of distribution.[27] On firmer ground, the minutes of evidence provide a rich pasture for the fiscal historian who is interested in the historical development of differentiation. The question of graduation was regarded by almost every witness, headed by J. S. Mill, with distaste as leading to 'confiscatory socialism'.[28] The twin proposals for differentiation and graduation were as old as the income tax itself. Not only was the latter accorded a place in the first income tax of 1799 but demands for differentiation between rentiers and industrialists were quickly made as that Bill was passing through the House in the last month of 1798.[29]

In Hume's committee the main burden of questions concerned exemptions and the insistence on this technical point was because economists and parliamentarians, like Mill and Hubbard, were concerned with the economic and moral principles of differentiation. Technically this meant exemptions and the charging of different tax rates, and the tax administrators were concerned with possible revenue losses if these were allowed.[30] As the whole of the working classes and many of the lower middle class were not liable to tax at this time, the tenor of the Hume inquiry developed through the 1850s into a struggle between landed, and professional and industrial interests, where injustice rather than actual hardship was the evil to be remedied.[31] By the time of the Hubbard committee the lines between 'precarious' and 'spontaneous' incomes[32]

26   The two main protagonists, Hume and Hubbard, died in 1855 and 1889 respectively. Differentiation was not introduced into the income tax until 1907.

27   See Sir Josiah C. Stamp, *British Incomes and Property* (London: King, 1920), also Phyllis Deane and W. A. Cole, *British Economic Growth: 1688-1959,* 2nd ed. (Cambridge: Cambridge University Press, 1967), App. 2, for comment on the relation of taxation to incomes in the Napoleonic war period.

28   Compare John Stuart Mill's acceptance of graduation in the succession duty with his rejection of the same principle in the income tax in, *Report from the Select Committee on Income and Property Tax,* 1861 (503), VII, Mins. of ev. qq. 3586 and 3597 (IUP National Finance: Income Tax 2), with his *Principles of Political Economy,* I, 7th ed. (London: Longmans, 1871), p. 82, and his restriction on the upper limit which might be taken in succession (ibid. II, p. 397).

29   See Basil E. V. Sabine, *A History of Income Tax* (London: Allen and Unwin, 1966), pp. 29-30.

30   The tax officials, Pressly and Timm, favoured reduction or abolition of exemptions, see, *Report from the Select Committee on Income and Property Tax,* 1861 (503), VII, Mins. of ev. qq. 82-8 (IUP National Finance: Income Tax 2).

31   Ibid. qq. 3203-423, where the meeting of the two worlds was eloquently described by three medical practitioners.

32   Also variously called: 'temporary', 'industrial', 'earned', and 'permanent', 'property', 'unearned'.

were tending almost to become identified with 'productive' and 'unproductive' activities,[33] At this point the discussion and the whole course of Hubbard's inquiry founded on the rock of classical economics. The fear of taxing capital, the 'engine of growth', warned against by Ricardo, translated one step backwards, became the danger of taxing savings.[34] As receivers of 'precarious' incomes were 'bound to save more' for future contingencies than the receivers of 'spontaneous' incomes, would it not be fair and economically appropriate to exempt the two classes *pro rata* with their *expected* savings? The remainder of the Hubbard report involved the reckless pursuit of this compounded misconception, with the luckless advocates (principally Newmarch and Hubbard) providing intellectually satisfying prey for interrogators such as Lowe.

Although it is easy to discern the hostility of the 1861 Public Expenditure Committee to its witnesses, the minutes of evidence reveal the difficulties of applying in practice the generalities of current theory in this period. For the historian of economic thought, Mill's evidence is of special interest. Nowhere in the course of his replies do we have a clear and unequivocal concept of Mill's idea of 'equality' in taxation.[35] The failure of the economic case against the allied front presented by the government, helped by its officials, had to wait upon small accretions to exemptions and allowances before the breakthrough of Harcourt's 1894 budget, when graduation, almost ignored by the two committees, was adopted for the death duties. The income tax continued, sporadically amended, until a firm political commitment to redistribution through fiscal means was made. This came when a Liberal government, freed from the shadow of Gladstone, implemented the recommendations of the Dilke committee of 1906 with almost irreverent haste.[36] Even then, in correct historical sequence, differentiation was brought into the income tax by Asquith in 1907, to be followed by graduation, introduced by Lloyd George, in 1909. At least one echo of these historical debates has survived in a modern tax controversy, i.e. that of wealth taxation,[37] and is a signal reminder that the

---

33   Hubbard suggested that Addington's schedules be abolished and the two divisions made: 'industrial' incomes—which could not exist apart from labour, and 'spontaneous' incomes—which were the unearned proceeds of invested property (ibid. Draft of Report by J. G. Hubbard, p.xiv).

34   See ibid. qq. 1296-1358 for a most searching examination of the 'savings/investment' principle by Cardwell.

35   See Gunnar Myrdal, *The Political Element in the Development of Economic Theory* (London: Routledge and Kegan Paul, 1953), pp. 156-90, also George Wirgman Hemming, *A Just Income Tax, how possible . . .* (London: 1852). Hemming was a witness before the Hume committee.

36   See *Select Committee on the Income Tax*, 1906 (365) IX, and also *Report of the Departmental Committee on Income Tax*, 1905 Cd. 2575 XLIV, chaired by Ritchie, chancellor of the exchequer in Balfour's government.

37   See *Report from the Select Committee on Income and Property Tax*, 1851 (563) X, Mins. of ev. qq. 4724-31.

terms, 'income', 'property', and 'capital' are far from being settled definitions in modern tax theory.

Government borrowings

Although for convenience, government borrowings are treated here as a separate category of government activity, it is unreal to regard them apart from the evolution of a fiscal and expenditure framework or from the financial system generally. Until well into the nineteenth century government borrowing was the only practical alternative to heavier, as opposed to more extensive, taxation and by the end of the eighteenth century the interest on the national debt had formed one half of government expenditure. In terms of income redistribution the amounts involved were substantial and in direction the flow was regressively towards the wealthier members of society.

The contribution of the financial system, as contrasted with the fiscal sector, as far as it includes government longer-term securities in the nineteenth century and before, is dealt with in the parliamentary papers on the national debt which were compiled after the great and successful conversion operation of 1888-89.[38] The 1898 report on the *History of Funded Debt, 1694-1786* [C.9010] LII was an act to complete the earlier report and the resulting historical record covers approximately 200 years of government activity in both Britain and Ireland.[39] The dividing line between the two reports is 1786 when the Commissioners for the National Debt were first appointed. Both the 1890-91 and 1898 reports supplied the bare bones of Hargreaves' history of the national debt,[40] and the profusion of skeletal remains include long series of financial statistics, lists of creations and redemptions of the debt, relevant statutes, references to parliamentary papers and debates, and some comments on financial schemes and mechanisms.

In using the 1898 report (dealing with the period 1694 to 1786) the historian must observe the warning that the early use of the phrase 'funded debt' applied to loans raised on the security of particular taxes and not, as in the modern sense, to perpetual debt.[41] Beyond some statistical

---

38   1890-91 [C.6539] XLVIII. These papers should be studied with the earlier *Notices of the various forms of the Public Debt, its Origin and Progress*, 1857-58 (443) XXXIII. The connection with *Reports from Commissioners appointed to investigate the drawing up and issuing of Exchequer Bills and on forged Exchequer Bills*, 1842 (1) and (409) XVIII (IUP National Finance: General 2) is obvious.

39   Some parts of the reports are antecedent to the period 1694 to 1890.

40   Eric L. Hargreaves, *The National Debt* (London: Frank Cass, 1966).

41   In the modern financial mechanism it is doubtful whether this distinction is really useful(see Hugh Dalton, *Principles of Public Finance* (London: Routledge and Kegan Paul, 1954), p. 177).

COMMENTARY

references to the land tax and the stamp duties the reports are fairly self-contained, though at the end of the 1891 report will be found some interesting data on loans to local authorities and the government's interposition of its superior credit facilities between these bodies and the securities market generally.[42]

Linkage between the establishment of the Bank of England and government debt is not pursued in detail in the 1898 report and for this, as well as for complementary statistics, the historian must turn to Clapham's *Bank of England*.[43] Similarly, the section in the 1891 report on savings banks has its modern revision in Horne's *History of Savings Banks*.[44] Generally, the space devoted, especially in the 1891 report, to different aspects of the national debt is quite uneven in the light of modern historical interest, e.g. compare the data given on sinking fund arrangements with the new policy on terminable annuities inaugurated by Gladstone in 1863.

The reports were compiled when, in spite of disturbing budget deficits and the threat of massive expenditure to come for anyone with a talent for prophecy, the debt and its charge were achieving record low levels in the century. It is as easy to detect the congratulatory air surrounding the reports as it is to disregard the debt today, yet the psychology of the debt remains eternal in some of its aspects.[45] The lotteries, abolished in the nineteenth century, have re-emerged as premium bonds and in the prophetic words of a writer in 1808, 'A spirit of adventure must be excited amongst the community, in order that Government may derive from it a pecuniary resource.'[46]

The use of the exchequer bill papers to the fiscal historian is a typical example of where he discards his familiar role of investigator and becomes a watcher at the feast. The papers are complementary but the main detective work was completed in the *Forged Exchequer Bills Report* of 1842. Perhaps their main value lies in an exposition of government credit in the money market in the period. The papers are additionally so self-contained as a nineteenth century case study that it is pertinent to recount the main details of the forgery.

42 *Report of the Proceedings of the Commissioners of the National Debt,* 1890-91 [C.6539] XLVIII, pp. 290-7 (IUP National Finance: General 7, pp. 298-305).

43 Sir John H. Clapham, *The Bank of England: A History,* 2 vols (Cambridge: Cambridge University Press, 1944).

44 H. Oliver Horne, *A History of Savings Banks* (Oxford: Oxford University Press, 1947).

45 Even physical in other aspects. Dalton pointed out that £496 millions of the debt contracted by 1817 was still oustanding in 1914 (H. Dalton, *Public Finance,* p. 179).

46 *Report of the Proceedings . . .* 1890-91 [C.6539] XLVIII 184 (IUP National Finance: General 7, p. 192).

Exchequer bills, government securities at the short end of the money market, had been introduced in 1696 in the turbulent genesis of modern government credit, for the 'more speedy answering of the Supplies',[47] It is interesting to note that the origin of the exchequer bill was due to a failure of government credit. The proposal for such a bill issue was a 'fail-safe' mechanism for the abortive National Land Bank of 1696.[48] In the very next year certain frauds by Knight, Burton, and others, which rocked the unsteady credit of the government, led William to promise that 'if they [the investing public] be cheated . . . it will be very hard.'[49] In 1707 the Bank of England was authorized to manage the circulation of exchequer bills and to fix the interest charges on them. This helped to develop loan relations between the Bank and the Treasury as well as providing the latter with an agency for the issue of a negotiable government security which was to become increasingly popular during the eighteenth century. By the early nineteenth century, the exchequer bill issue had reached its peak and the bills were issued for many purposes other than simply general supply.[50]

More trouble and forgeries came to light in 1823 and 1824[51] but it was in 1841 that Beaumont Smith, an exchequer clerk of 21 years' service, decided to issue fraudulent duplicates of 377 Supply Bills. With the help of his confederate, Ernest Rapallo, Smith raised huge loans in the city on the security of the bills and city panic ensued in October 1841. Supply bills were issued twice a year and the forgeries concerned bills issued in March and June 1841. The bills ran for a year and forgeries were almost bound to be discovered by the time that the bills were returned for funding or for payment. Rapallo confessed totally and was set free, but it went 'very hard' with Smith who was transported for life in 1842. The ground had been prepared by Smith himself who, to make the issue more

---

47   7 and 8 Wm. III, c. 6 (Public Accounts).

48   See R. D. Richards, 'The Exchequer Bill in English Government Finance', *Economic History,* III, no. 11 (1936), pp. 193-211.

49   Treasury minute dated 20 November 1697, quoted as Appendix 6 of the *Report from Commissioners appointed to investigate the Drawing up and Issuing of Exchequer Bills and on Forged Exchequer Bills,* 1842 (1) XVIII (IUP National Finance: General 2).

50   By the 1840s, for example, several kinds of exchequer bills were being raised to finance West India Relief, Public Works and Fisheries, etc., but Supply bills formed the greatest proportion. Only bills on Supply continued after 1846.

51   About £17,000 was lost in these years. The paper, design, and printing of the bills had barely altered by 1840, and these were of poor quality. Only the denominations had changed (they were, in 1842, £50, £100, £200, £500 and £1,000) i.e. forgery was even more attractive. A photograph of an early exchequer bill is given in Peter G. M. Dickson, *The Financial Revolution in England* (London: Macmillan, 1967), opp. p. 395.

secure, had in 1834 gained acceptance of his own scheme to concentrate the preparation of bills in his own hands.[52]

The 1842 *Exchequer Bills* and *Forged Exchequer Bills* Reports included in the papers are clearly of most use to the financial historian and they contain much information which has not been embodied in secondary authorities.[53] The 160 witnesses produced evidence which throws detailed light on the position of the Bank of England in the money market, on dealings on the stock exchange and various banking houses, as well of course, on the practice and process of issue by the Exchequer Office. They also offer information into the state of liquidity of the money market, discounting, parcelling of bill portfolios, and the life of bills as they were held to maturity by different persons and institutions. By the time of the exchequer forgeries in 1841, the exchequer bill had already begun its long years of decline.The commercial bill of exchange was more popular at least by the late 1820s and its flexibility and counter-attraction to the money market after 1833[54] increased still further. Reform had been a paramount need not only in the Issue Office, but in the exchequer bills themselves, for, after the 1830s, short-term government borrowing was largely affected through Ways and Means on the Consolidated Fund series, and consols themselves were being used mainly for 'open market' operations.[55]

The most modern *tour de force* on the management of the money market in the later seventeenth and eighteenth centuries is to be found in Dickson's study.[56] It may be noted that the functions of the exchequer were the receipt and issue of public money, but a revision of the system in 1834 had confined the preliminary issue to the Issue Office of the exchequer. From the exchequer, bills went to the public via the Paymaster's Office, then to the government broker. Other bills went to the Bank of England and to other departments of the government. The historical record reveals least for this latter category of departmental holdings. The Issue Office of the exchequer was only one branch of the exchequer and it came under the control of the Comptroller of the Exchequer, a post established in 1835, made independent of the government and responsible to parliament. Control of issues was thus

52   He was promoted to senior clerk later that year for his services.

53   For example, William M. Scammell, *The London Discount Market* (London: Elek, 1968) and Sir John H. Clapham, *The Bank of England: A History,* 2 vols (Cambridge: Cambridge University Press, 1944).

54   The 1833 Act freed three months' bills of exchange from the limitations of the usury laws.

55   Further details are given in Richard S. Sayers, *Central Banking After Bagehot* (Oxford: Clarendon Press, 1957), especially chapter 5.

56   Peter G. M. Dickson, *Financial Revolution in England* (London: Macmillan, 1967).

'insulated from both politics and the government'.[57] When the Audit Board was merged with the exchequer in 1866 the post became the Comptroller and Auditor General.

The management of government expenditure

The control of government over its revenues had always been more sharply focussed and contested in the history of the long struggle for parliamentary financial control. Control of expenditure, after the initial victory by parliament over the monarch, had withered until the nineteenth century assault by interested and courageous spirits such as Joseph Hume, Francis Baring and Henry Parnell. It was in the nature of expenditure that this should be so, politically, because the strength of departmental and interested parliamentary groups were strong forces to be reckoned with (e.g. the financial battle of Wellington in 1830 if lost, had shown the strength of entrenched opposition) and, technically, because the items in question were many and they included capital payments intractably disbursed by most departments over long periods of years.

Broadly, the evolutionary pattern and the predictable wishes of any spending department were to achieve independence in auditing its own accounts, retaining its own balances, and having maximum flexibility over its aggregate expenditure. In short, the desire was to avoid the interference of parliament and to achieve a near *laissez-faire* situation within the government bureaucracy. As that 'ferocious economist' Ralph Lingen expressed it to the *Select Committee on Civil Service Expenditure* in 1873, 'Each department under each Minister is almost a little kingdom in itself.'[58] Perhaps the most flagrant abuse of individualism linked expenditure and revenue. Lord Monteagle, Comptroller General of the Exchequer since 1839 expressed traditional doubts in 1848 of the propriety of reform when £7 millions were known to have been spent and nearly £2 millions received by departments without any knowledge of his own department.[59] The self-imposed task of parliament in the second and third quarters of the nineteenth century was to devise checks to control this system, not only to avoid the wastage of funds through extravagance but the loss incurred by multiple holdings of idle balances. Above all, it strove to ensure a proper accountability to the nation through itself and to levy the minimum burden of taxation compatible with efficiency.

57   Basil Chubb, *The Control of Public Expenditure* (Oxford: Clarendon Press, 1952), p. 13.

58   *Select Committee on Civil Services Expenditure,* 1873 (352) VII, mins. of ev. q. 2911 (IUP National Finance: General 5).

59   *Select Committee on Miscellaneous Expenditure,* 1847-48 (543), XVIII, Part I, mins. of ev. qq. 2547 and 2549 (IUP National Finance: General 3).

The basic tools of necessary reforms were proper accounting procedures including the double entry system of accounts and consistent fiscal periods amenable to the check of an audit. Competent estimating under Treasury guidance, appropriation, accounting checks and final audit could not exist without these preliminaries to control. The efficient staff and effective methods of working necessary to promote reformation hardly existed before the mid-century.

The period before 1850 was replete with suggestions for revising control of expenditures and the *Select Committee on Public Monies* of 1856[60] made the most cogent recommendations for an overhaul of the existing framework. Although the *Select Committee on Miscellaneous Expenditure* of 1848 made no specific proposals for reform it evoked a renewed response in those who regretted the passing of the 'economy' movement of recent past years. The genesis of 'miscellaneous' expenditure was to be found in the complete separation of the Civil List in 1831 from the expenses of civil government and by the mid-century the latter had grown to over 100 votes divided into five classes of estimates. Reclassification was carried out intermittently as new items of expenditure arose, with the objective of confining the classes of spending to residual items. In this type of expenditure, hall-marked by sudden urgency and unforeseen contingencies, government finance, according to a recent writer, 'covered for many years a multitude of unspecified sins of extravagance.'[61] A substantial proportion of miscellaneous payments went abroad and a heavy element of capital items was included in the categories of classes.[62] Rises in some of the categories of expenditure since 1800 had caused alarm and a demand for control, but particular sources of irritation were the difficulties of securing estimates from a large variety of sources in time for the yearly government budget and accounting for expenditure on capital projects spread over a number of years. The wide extent of reference of the Miscellaneous Expenditure select committees itself debilitated their efficiency and their 1860 report[63] brought their activities to an end.

Efficiency factors came to the fore when Trevelyan revealed his

60 *Report of the Select Committee on Public Monies,* 1856 (375), XV, 1857 (107 Session 1), II and (279 Session 2), IX.

61 Paul Einzig, *The Control of the Purse* (London: Secker and Warburg, 1959), p. 163.

62 The number of classes in 'miscellaneous' payments, relabelled 'civil estimates' in accordance with a recommendation of the 1847-48 Select Committee Report XVIII (543) Part I, p. viii, had reached eight by 1855 (see Maurice Wright, *Treasury Control of the Civil Service, 1854-74* [Oxford: Clarendon Press, 1969] Appendix V, p. 374).

63 *Select Committee on Miscellaneous Expenditure,* 1860 (483), IX (IUP National Finance: General 4).

proposals to the 1847-48 committee for the division of departmental work into mechanical and intellectual.[64] His views found little favour with other witnesses but by the early 1850s his ideas, diluted by less spartan logic, had been accepted into the Treasury and the Colonial Office.[65] Retrenchment on efficiency grounds was uppermost in the deliberations of the *Select Committee on Civil Service Expenditure, Third Report* of 1873, when the committee took evidence on copying machines in departments. William Baxter, Lowe's Financial Secretary, enthusiastically called for 'copying presses' from which he calculated savings of up to £300,000 per annum and the redundancy of at least 2,000 clerks[66]—claims which would have delighted George Downing or Sir William Coventry, Treasury innovators of two centuries past.

The civil services expenditures on staffing however, were still proving intractable by the time the 1873 Select Committee had met to review the items over which the Treasury had not 'direct or effectual control'. For other departments of state, control had largely been defined by minutes or by acts which required full accounts of appropriation and expenditure. Such control had long since been technically present in the Navy department in 1832, after Graham's sweeping suggestions, and had been extended to the War Office in 1846, to the Office of Woods and Works in 1851, and to the revenue departments in 1861. For the civil services, control was mostly a matter of administrative custom or 'moral suasion'. In this committee's discussions was more than a hint of Gladstone's dissatisfaction with Treasury power when an amendment proposed that '. . . the Committee learned with painful surprise that it is a "delusion" to believe that the Treasury does now exercise a direct and effectual control over the expenditure of the country . . .' and that '. . . this impotency or lack of administrative power in the Treasury deserves . . . the serious attention of the Legislature.'[67] The words were refused insertion by a vote of 7 to 5. The formal provisions of the Exchequer and Audit Act of 1866[68] had still some years to run before their prop and support. the Public Accounts Committee. could inspire respect for that 'enlightened tyrant', the Treasury.

Until proper accounts and appropriation procedures had become

64   *Select Committee* . . . 1847-48 (543) XVIII, Part I, pp. 113-4.

65   Of a large number of studies devoted to later civil service reform, see M. Wright, *Treasury Control* . . . (Oxford: Clarendon Press, 1969), pp. 53-193, and for a valuable summary, Edward Hughes, 'Civil Service Reform 1853-55', *History*, New Series, XXVII (1942), pp. 51-83.

66   *Select Committee* . . . 1873 (352) VII, mins. of ev. qq. 4649-50.

67   Ibid., pp. xvi-xvii.

68   29 and 30 Vict. c. 39 (Exchequer and Audit Depts.).

technically possible and legislatively obligatory a Public Accounts Committee could not perform the function of a watchdog on permitted spending. However premature the establishment of this committee might have seemed in 1861, its effective future was guaranteed by Baring and Northcote, both of whom were promptly named as the first members. Its first five reports (IUP National Finance: General 4) fulfilled Gladstone's faith in its future and its permanent place in parliament's financial machinery was assured in the next year by a Standing Order of the Commons.[69]

The objects of local authorities' capital expenditure and the sources of the funds which they used are largely unknown in economic history, at least before 1868.[70] This is quite deplorable as it is clear that total local government expenditure was rising much faster proportionally than that of the central government during the second half of the nineteenth century. Future investigation of this deficiency must rest largely with local and regional research, in the first instance with representative indexes of capital formation in the boroughs and the counties.[71] So far as central government grants were concerned (local authorities used the proceeds of the rate funds as well as private loans on the mortgage of the rates) advances against capital investment were important certainly after the Napoleonic wars. The Board of Commissioners, created in 1817, regularized the *ad hoc* provision of loans to certain local authorities by their power to advance money on the security of exchequer bills,[72] and this was replaced in 1843 by the Public Works Loan Fund which ceased to lend via exchequer bills and drew directly from the Consolidated Fund. The latter body was the only public agency standing between the local authorities and the private capital market.

The Select Committee of 1875[73] was given the task of considering legislation passed since 1817 in the light of imminent amendment and consolidation bills. The amendment bill was the most important item as it sought to take powers of varying the rate of interest on loans and that of compounding debts from the Treasury which had acted as a court of

69 For an authoritative account of the committee see Basil Chubb, *The Control of Public Expenditure* (Oxford: Clarendon Press, 1952), pp. 23-41.

70 See *Report of G. J. Goschen on the Increase of Local Taxation with especial reference to the proportion of Local and Imperial Burdens borne by the different classes of Real Property*, 1870, IV (470).

71 See Derek Gregory, 'The Public Accounts of the County of Lancashire from 1820 to 1889' (unpublished MA thesis, University of Leeds, 1966).

72 M. W. Flinn, 'The Poor Employment Act of 1817', *Economic History Review*, XIV, no. 1 (1961), pp. 82-92.

73 *Select Committee on Public Works Loan Acts Amendment Bill*, 1875 (358), XIV (IUP National Finance: General 5).

appeal for borrowing authorities. Percentage rises in local spending on health and education in the 1870s and the official absence on limit to individual loans had sown fears of a spending spree by local authorities and the point of the amendment bill was to promote a stricter sense of the need for economy. Although the total yearly amounts were really small they, like the estimates for civil expenditure, were a worry to the chancellor and tended to upset the budget unless requirements were known well in advance. The significant point brought out by this select committee was the desire of chancellor Northcote to see 'local budgetting', i.e. self-sufficient local authorities dealing with a largely independent body like the Public Works Loan Commissioners on something like a market footing instead of 'grasping at the Consolidated Fund'. Neither did Welby show any enthusiasm for Treasury responsibility for this area of government commitment. One bill, not two, passed into law, the Public Works Loans Act of 1875.[74] The Commission which the Act established was placed under the regulatory control of the Treasury which was given power to vary bargains with local authorities, and the annual amount available for loans from the budget was revised each year. The powers and discretion of this body have largely survived to the present day.

The case of Ireland

The case of Ireland provided Britain with a range of problems in colonization which, after the legislative union in 1801, became exercises in regionalism. Into the field of fiscal relations was carried the running sore of 'disaffection' which had plagued relations since the 'planting' policy of the seventeenth century and had led Petty to proclaim of Ireland that 'if you are conquered all is lost; or if you conquer, yet you are subject to swarms of thieves and robbers.'[75] In its efforts to establish capitalist agriculture and raise the productivity from a 'potato economy' the classical solution for Ireland in the nineteenth century was to provide essential public works as a basis for future growth not as an immediate palliative for unemployment. This immediately presented the rooted objection to public expenditure, that funds might be embezzled or, at second best, be regarded as a substitute for private initiative. Precedents were too numerous for such worries to be taken lightly and this attitude goes a good way to explaining the general classical opposition to government spending, but not to 'good' government. Ireland was no exception and 'there was in fact something of a tradition in Ireland ... that public works and jobbery went hand in hand, and that every man of

74   38 and 39 Vict. c. 89 (Public Works Loans).
75   Ed. Charles Henry Hull, *The Economic Writings of Sir William Petty*, I (Cambridge: Cambridge University Press, 1899), p. 46.

any influence did his best to get whatever pickings he could from public expenditure.'[76]

Nevertheless, Ireland was a special case. With her destitute and unresponsive agriculture and 'the inevitability of the absentee landlord wringing his rents from misery'[77] she provoked sympathy for public infusion of funds from no less a classicist than Nassau Senior, like Petty an eye witness of the Irish scene. Fifteen years before the great famine it was clear to Senior that 'the failure of a crop is not a contingency against which a labouring man can be expected to make a provision . . . public relief therefore could not be said to come in lieu of ordinary charity.'[78] Details, reports and statistics of how famine in Ireland attracted public expenditure under the supreme command of C. E. Trevelyan, the personification of Victorian moral rectitude and industry, abound in the parliamentary papers on famine in Ireland (IUP Famine: Ireland 1-8).[79] The complementary issue of Irish tax husbandry did not achieve serious attention until it became clear from the 1850s that efforts to raise Irish productivity, and consequently taxable income and expenditure, had been defeated. Irish taxation and her apportionment of national debt had been temporarily settled in 1800 before the immense rise in the debt had led to a consolidation of British and Irish exchequers in 1817. At that time the Irish income per head was almost 65 per cent of the British figure.[80] This relative figure declined, in spite of even greater proportionate decline in the population, and Irish taxable capacity also had fallen. In pursuit of 'fiscal equity' Gladstone extended his 'temporary' income tax to Ireland in 1853 and his equalisation of the spirit duties in 1858 imposed extra burdens which even dissenting members of the Royal Commission of 1895 agreed were not supportable.[81] This action was undertaken in the

76   R. D. Collison Black, 'The Classical View of Ireland's Economy' in *The Classical Economists and Economic Policy,* ed. A. W. Coats (London: Methuen, 1971), p. 99. For a political comment on the misapplication of public funds in Ireland, see 'Local Government and Ireland' in *The Radical Programme* by Joseph Chamberlain and Others (London: Chapman and Hall, 1885), chapter 9.

77   Nassau Senior, *Letter to Lord Howick on a legal provision for the Irish Poor, commutation of tithes, and a provision for the Irish Roman Catholic Clergy* (London, 1831), p. 26.

78   Ibid., p. 21.

79   See, for example, *Correspondence on Measures adopted by the Government for Relief of Distress,* 1846 (735), XXXVII, 1847 (761) and (56) LI (IUP Famine: Ireland 5); also his evidence to the *Select Committee on Miscellaneous Expenditure,* 1847-48 (543), XVIII, Pt. I, mins. of ev. qq. 4854-5204 (IUP National Finance: General 3, pp. 444-73).

80   Phyllis Deane, 'Contemporary Estimates of National Income in the first half of the nineteenth century', *Economic History Review,* VIII, no. 3 (1956), pp. 339-54.

81   *Royal Commission on Financial Relations between Great Britain and Ireland,* 1896 [C.8262], XXXIII (IUP National Finance: General 6, Final Report).

face of protest, without inquiry into Ireland's taxable capacity on Gladstone's part.[82]

Amongst the discussions on Irish affairs undertaken in the conciliatory mood of the later nineteenth century was Giffen's pertinent essay on Irish parliamentary representation.[83] Giffen pointed out that if the representation of Ireland in the imperial parliament was to remain at anything like the current figure of 105 members from a total of 658, then that country should bear an additional tax burden of 50 per cent on its present tax revenue contribution. In this impossible circumstance, Giffen proposed the alternative logic that Irish over-representation 'a substantial mischief to the whole United Kingdom' should be cut. This timely linkage of politics and finance, in the same decade as the Home Rule movement was first launched, was not re-emphasized until Giffen's second essay[84] repeated the connection. On the second occasion the controversy invoked by Giffen's remarks contributed to the appointment of Childers' commission in 1894. By the time the long demanded royal commission had supplied its final report Childers was dead and Gladstone's second home rule had disappeared into oblivion.

The terms of reference of the commission were quite impossible to answer with any degree of objective precision for several reasons. The terms were: (1) to determine the standards and principles of comparison for determining equitably the relative capacities of Britain and Ireland to bear taxation, (2) further, to determine the true proportions of taxable capacity and (3) to detail the history of financial relations between the two countries since 1800. In an attempt to answer the third term the efforts of such famous officials as Welby, Milner and Hamilton were pitted against the elusive and often non-existent figures of Irish duties and the intricacies of their separation.[85] Differences in the respective economies and social patterns ensured that 'principles and specific standards' of taxable capacity were not to be found in 'equalisation', nor did the commission find agreement in any alternative principles.

Reform had eventually to wait on World War I, but as well as affording incomparable statistics and information on government policy in Ireland,

82   *Hansard*, 3 ser. 24 February 1865.

83   Sir Robert Giffen, *Economic Inquiries and Studies*, I (London: Bell, 1904), 'The Taxation and Representation of Ireland', pp. 277-81. Originally published in *The Economist*, XXXIV, no. 1710 (3 June 1876), pp. 653-4.

84   Ibid. 'The Economic Value of Ireland to Great Britain', pp. 431-55. Originally published in the *Nineteenth Century*, XIX, no. 109 (March 1886), pp. 329-45.

85   H. W. Chisholm had previously attempted this task in 1864 and presented his results to the *Select Committee on the Taxation of Ireland*, 1864 (513), XV and 1865 (330), XII.

the whole inquiry (published in the reports of the royal commissions in 1895 and 1896) put to the test many of the problems of redressing regional imbalance in two economies moving rapidly in opposite directions. It was a nineteenth century faith in the efficacy of taxation, as well as Irish belligerency, which led O'Brien (a member of the Irish Land Commission) to claim that English taxation policy had prevented the growth of the Irish economy at the same time as it had helped to lay the foundations of England's nineteenth century wealth.[86]

86 *Royal Commission on Financial Relations between Great Britain and Ireland,* 1895 [C.7720-1], XXXVI, Appendix II, p. 385 (IUP National Finance: General 6, p. 479).

The Documents

NATIONAL FINANCE AND INCOME TAX

The dates of these Parliamentary Papers range from 1840 to the end of the nineteenth century but the coverage of the statistics, statutes, history and the wealth of miscellaneous notation carries back the story of government finances very much earlier. The older phrase 'national finance' has more recently been relabelled 'public finance' to avoid confusion with the modern preoccupation with national and social accounting. The 'financial' aspect is however, still liable to misinterpretation in the light of the groupings followed in these papers. Broadly, the papers are concerned with the revenues, expenditures, and administration of government. Revenues are conceived of as embracing the main areas of direct and indirect taxation and the proceeds of government credit instruments which comprised the long and short term debt. Expenditure ranges over a vast array of government services too long to be catalogued except in the papers themselves. The administration of government financial business is chiefly noted in the light of control through the audit and in the accountability of funds. Territorially, the papers are extended by one volume to illustrate the shaping force of British financial hegemony over Ireland in the nineteenth century.

This specialist area of British economic development in the nineteenth century has its own problems of fragmentation and the coverage in these volumes is necessarily selective. Monetary policy, for example, has been grouped separately and is dealt with elsewhere in this volume, but students will readily appreciate the intimate connection of that sector with that of the sets under review here.

National Finance: General 1 Report from the select committee on import duties together with the first report from the commissioners on the collection and management of the revenue, 1840-42. (416 pp.)

The main report in this volume deals with the famous 1840 inquiry into the effects and desirability of the tariff system on British economic development at a time when industrial and commercial growth was straining to break the remnants of government regulation and constriction.

Evidence was taken from officials of the Board of Trade, representatives of chambers of commerce, manufacturers and merchants giving extensive information on the nature, extent and effects of Britain's tariffs.

In addition the tariff systems of continental countries were examined. A considerable section of evidence was devoted to the corn laws and to other articles of commerce which illustrated the case for free trade. A lengthy appendix provides tabulated information on the effects of duties on a long list of articles being used as raw materials in British industry.

The first report of the commissioners on the collection and management of revenue dealt with the 'emporium' of Liverpool.

Original references

1840	(601) V	Import Duties, Sel. Cttee. Rep., mins of ev., appendix, index.
1842	[400] XXV	Collection and management of revenue, R. Com. 1st Rep.

National Finance: General 2 Reports from commissioners appointed to investigate the drawing up and issuing of exchequer bills and on forged exchequer bills, 1842. (648 pp. 1 folding table)

This volume deals with the action taken in 1842 to examine the Issue Office of the Exchequer consequent on the discovery of certain frauds in the issue of exchequer bills in the previous year, despite the remodelling of this Department in 1834. The report of the 1842 commission investigated the mechanism and process of issue, and the later report deals with the short history of the forgeries.

Original references

1842	(1) XVIII	Exchequer bills, R. Com. Rep., mins. of ev., appendices.
	[409]	Forged exchequer bills, R. Com. Rep., mins. of ev., appendix.

National Finance: General 3 Report from the select committee on miscellaneous expenditure with minutes of evidence, appendices and index, 1847-48. (1,104 pp.)

In this volume the reports and minutes of evidence of the committee of 1847-48 on the seven classes of miscellaneous expenditure are printed. The committee, which inquired into possible economies in these accounts and into the method of appropriation, included Gladstone, Kay-Shuttleworth, C. E. Trevelyan and H. Labouchere. The coverage included the years from 1800 but expenditure statistics are mainly confined to the period 1838-48. The classes of expenditure included items such as the salaries of government officials, court expenses, secret and consular services, poor law services, assistance to captured slaves, and items on capital account.

Original references

1847-48 (543) XVIII Pt. 1		Miscellaneous expenditure, Sel. Cttee. Rep., mins. of ev., Part 1.
	(543-II) Pt. II	Miscellaneous expenditure, Sel. Cttee, Rep., mins. of ev., appendices, Part II.
	(543)	Miscellaneous expenditure, Sel. Cttee. Rep., index.

National Finance: General 4   Reports from select committees on miscellaneous expenditure, the auditing of public accounts and charges on foreign trade with minutes of evidence, appendices and indices, 1860-62. (680 pp. 1 folding coloured map)

This volume contains the report of a further select committee appointed in 1860 to examine expenditure on miscellaneous services and to advise on the possibility of reducing it, five reports from a select committee appointed in 1861 to examine from year to year the audited accounts of public expenditure, and the report of a select committee on the charges imposed on exports and imports by the 1860 Customs Act.

The importance of the 1861 Public Accounts Committee was indicated by the eminence of its personnel: Sir Stafford Northcote, Sir Francis Baring, Sir James Graham, Richard Cobden and others.

Original references

1860	(483) IX	Miscellaneous expenditure, Sel. Cttee. Rep., mins of ev., appendices.
	(483-1)	Miscellaneous expenditure, Sel. Cttee. Rep., index.
1861	(329) XI	Audited Accounts of the public expenditure, Sel. Cttee. 1st Rep., mins of ev., appendices.
	(367)	Audited accounts of the public expenditure, Sel. Cttee. 2nd Rep.
	(418)	Audited accounts of the public expenditure, Sel. Cttee. 3rd Rep.
	(448)	Audited accounts of the public expenditure, Sel. Cttee. 4th Rep.
	(468)	Audited accounts of the public expenditure, Sel. Cttee. 5th Rep.
	(468-1)	Audited accounts of the public expenditure, Sel. Cttee. index to the five reps.
1862	(429) XII	Charges on foreign trade (Customs Act, 1860), Sel. Cttee. Rep., mins. of ev., appendices, index.

National Finance: General 5   Reports from select committees on civil service expenditure and the Public Works Loans Acts

Amendment Bill and committee reports on public accounts, with minutes of evidence, appendices and indices, 1873-76. (832 pp.)

The three reports of a select committee appointed to advise on whether reductions could be made in expenditure for civil services (other than the National Debt and Civil List) and to examine especially the branches of expenditure not under the control of the treasury make up the largest section of this volume.

The other papers in the volume are the three reports submitted by the standing committee on public accounts in 1876 and a special report from the 1875 *Select Committee on the Public Works Loan Acts Amendment Bill*. The public accounts reports examined the accounts for the seven classes of civil services, the army appropriation account, the revenue departments' accounts (customs, posts and telegraphs) and several other accounts of lesser importance.

Original references

1873	(131) VII	Civil Services expenditure, Sel. Cttee. Rep.
	(248)	Civil Services expenditure, Sel. Cttee. 2nd Rep.
	(352)	Civil Services expenditure, Sel. Cttee. 3rd Rep., mins. of ev., appendices, index.
1875	(358) XIV	The Public Works Loans Acts Amendment Bill, Sel. Cttee. Rep., mins. of ev., appendices, index.
1876	(133) VIII	Public Accounts, Cttee. 1st Rep., mins. of ev., appendix.
	(207)	Public Accounts, Cttee. 2nd Rep., mins. of ev., appendix.
	(324)	Public Accounts, Cttee. 3rd Rep., mins. of ev., appendix, index.

National Finance: General 6   Reports from the select committee and royal commission and memoranda on the financial relations between Great Britain and Ireland with minutes of evidence, appendices and indices, 1890-96. (1,120 pp.)

This volume contains the 1890 Select Committee Report on the financial relations between England, Scotland and Ireland, the 1895-96 Royal Commission Report on the financial relations between Great Britain and Ireland, and memoranda from the Treasury, and Customs and Inland Revenue Departments on the same subject.

The bulk of the volume is taken up with the 1895-96 commission, chaired by Hugh C. E. Childers (a former chancellor of the exchequer) until his death in 1895. The commission collected extensive oral, documentary and statistical evidence but it failed to agree on many aspects of the inquiry and dissenting views were contained in eight minority reports which cover the history of financial relations between the two countries from Grattan's parliament in the 1780s to 1890.

Original references

1890	(412) XIII	Financial relations (England, Scotland and Ireland), Sel. Cttee. Rep., mins. of ev., appendices, index.
1890-91	(329) XLVIII	Financial relations between England, Scotland and Ireland, Memo by Treasury, Customs and Inland Revenue Departments.
1894	(313) LI	Amounts contributed by Great Britain and Ireland to the imperial revenue, Treasury memo.
1895	[C.7720] XXXVI	Financial relations between Great Britain and Ireland, R. Com. 1st Rep.
	[C.7720-1]	Financial relations between Great Britain and Ireland, R. Com., mins. of ev.
1896	[C.8008] XXXIII	Financial relations between Great Britain and Ireland, R. Com., mins. of ev.
	[C.8262]	Financial relations between Great Britain and Ireland, R. Com. Final Rep.

National Finance: General 7 Report from the comptroller general on the proceedings of the national debt commissioners from 1786 to 1890 together with a report on the history of the funded debt from 1694 to 1786, 1890-98. (416 pp 1 folding table)

The two papers in this volume provide an account of the history of the British national debt from 1694 to 1890. The 1890 paper, based on the original records of the Public Records Offices of England and Ireland, was the work of A. T. King, Chief Clerk of the National Debt Office. It describes the development of the national debt from 1694 until the time when the National Debt Commissioners were established in 1786. The 1890-91 paper takes up the investigation and the description of the growth of the debt ends in 1890.

Original references

1890-91	[C.6539] XLVIII	National Debt, Rep. of the Comptroller General to the National Debt Commissioners on their proceedings from their commencement in 1786 to the present time.
1898	[C.9010] LII	History of the earlier years of the funded debt, from 1694 to 1786.

National Finance: General 8 Reports on the customs and tariffs of the United Kingdom from 1800 to 1897 with notes on the more important branches of receipts from 1660, 1898. (960 pp.)

This volume includes a comprehensive and well-ordered account of the history of British customs and tariffs from 1660 to 1897, together with some information on customs revenue and the law relating to it before 1660. It was compiled by T. J. Pittar, a senior official in the Statistics Office of the Customs House. The remainder of the report consists of 500 pages of tables giving, in full, the duties payable on all articles of merchandise for each year from 1823 (the year in which duties between England and Ireland were equalized) up to 1897. The appendix has important additional information, e.g. a synopsis of older laws on importation, exportation and customs going back to the reign of Henry III. Apart from the general index the volume has an index of articles, then and previously subject to duty, with the dates at which repealed duties ceased.

Original reference

1898 [C.8706] LXXXV   Customs tariffs of the United Kingdom from 1800 to 1897 with some notes on the more important branches of receipts from the year 1660, appendices, indices.

National Finance: Income Tax 1 Reports from the select
committee on income and property tax with minutes of
evidence, appendices and indices, 1851-52. (1,036 pp. 4
folding charts [2 coloured])

This volume, the Hume report, provides a mid-century view of the
organization and methods of the Inland Revenue and, as well as its
distinguished chairman, it included other eminent figures such as Disraeli,
Roebuck, Cobden and Baring. Evidence given by John Stuart Mill and
William Farr gives a first hand account of economic opinion on the income
tax in this period. Comparative evidence on the tax codes of the United
States and Texas was heard by the committee and the reports include a
short history of the income tax since its introduction in 1799.

Original references

1851	(563) X	Income and Property Tax, Sel. Cttee. Rep.
1852	(354) IX	Income and Property Tax, Sel. Cttee. 1st Rep., mins. of ev.
	(510)	Income and Property Tax, Sel. Cttee. 2nd Rep., mins. of ev.

National Finance: Income Tax 2 Report from the select
committee on the mode of assessing and collecting income
and property tax, with minutes of evidence, appendix and
index 1861. (400 pp.)

This volume, the Hubbard report, marks the second and last report on
proposals to reform the income tax in the nineteenth century. With
Hubbard in the chair, the committee included two future chancellors of
the exchequer, Sir Stafford Northcote and Robert Lowe. Gladstone, the
chancellor of the day, took an active part in the inquiry and the evidence
reproduced is a signal of his hostility and of the aversion to the scheme of
Gladstone's specially selected committee members.

Original references

1861	(503) VII	Income and Property Tax, Sel. Cttee. Rep. and appendix.
	(503-1)	Income and Property Tax, Sel. Cttee. Index.

Bibliography

The most recent general work on the history of the income tax is Basil E. V. Sabine, *A History of the Income Tax* (London: Allen and Unwin, 1966), but the latest and most detailed work to deal with the parliamentary papers on income tax is Fakhri Shehab, *Progressive Taxation*, (Oxford: Clarendon Press, 1953) which conveniently allots one chapter to each of the reports, i.e. chapter 6 deals with Hume's committee, and chapter 8 with the Hubbard committee. The intervening chapter takes up the debate between Disraeli and Gladstone (who were each members of the respective committees) and in this respect the important contributions, John Gotham Maitland, *Property and Income Tax, Shedule A and Shedule D* (London: 1852), and J. G. Hubbard's *Reform or Reject the Income Tax: Objections to a Reform of the Income Tax considered in Two Letters to the Editor of* The Times; *with Additional Notes* (London: 1853) are properly included.

A fuller recitation of Charles Babbage's objections to the reformist case is found in his *Thoughts on the Principles of Taxation with reference to a Property Tax* (London: Murray, 1848) and reprinted in 1851, in which that strangely inventive thinker expounds his annual 'class benefit' basis of taxation in a static economy. Mill's *Principles* is obviously essential as authoritative contemporary tax theory and from an abundant collection of writings on the free trade connection the tracts of the Liverpool Financial Reform Association provide the extreme viewpoint for the reformist faction. The parliamentary papers themselves, however, are the best forum for debate on how taxation theory could be translated into administrative practice, and one notable exercise is the discussion, in the 1852 *Income and Property Tax 2nd Report,* on the plan for capitalizing incomes which held the imagination of tax theorists for some time to come. For the broad view of parliamentarians during the last century, Valerie Cromwell's 'Changing Parliamentary attitudes to income tax in the nineteenth century', *XIIe Congrès International des Sciences Historiques. Etudes presentees a la Commission Internationale pour L'Histoire des Assemblees d'Etats,* XXI (Vienna: 1965; reprint, Nauwelaerts, Paris, 1966), pp. 35-42, will be found useful. A modern comment on the possibility of taxing wages at source in the mid-century will be found in Olive Anderson, 'Wage-earners and Income Tax: a mid-nineteenth century discussion', *Public Administration,* XLI (Summer 1963), 189-92.

Amongst a mass of parliamentary papers relating to taxation and overseas trade some useful additional material will be found in *Returns relating to Imports and Exports,* 1863, LXVI (1) and *Customs Tariffs of the United Kingdom,* 1898 [C.8706] LXXXV (IUP National Finance: General 8). The student of the parliamentary papers 1840, V (601) and 1842, XXV (400) will perhaps view customs records earlier than the eighteenth century only with marginal interest. In this he will not be unduly tempted as the accidental destruction of records has restricted most research to the post-1696 period, and ample secondary works exist to satisfy interest in the eighteenth century. Among these are the classic studies: Elizabeth E. Hoon, *The Organization of the English Customs System: 1696-1786* (Newton Abbot: David and Charles, 1968), originally published in 1938; George Norman Clark, *Guide to English Commercial Statistics, 1696-1782* (London: Royal Historical Society Guides and Handbooks, no. 1, 1938), and E. B. Schumpeter, *English Overseas Trade Statistics, 1697-1808* (Oxford: Oxford University Press, 1960). For works covering the nineteenth century, the recognized general authority is Albert H. Imlah, *Economic Elements in the Pax Britannica* (Cambridge, Mass.: Harvard University Press, 1958) which has the refinement of assessing the balance of payments figures. In this connection it is worth looking at Imlah's 'British Balance of Payments and Export of Capital, 1816-1913', *Economic History Review*, V, no. 2 (1952), pp. 208-32. Another study, of somewhat lesser stature, is Weiner Schlöte, *British Overseas Trade from 1700 to the 1930s* (Oxford: Blackwell, 1952). The difficulties and inconsistencies in the statistics are taken further in A. Maizels, 'The Overseas Trade Statistics of the United Kingdom', *Journal of the Royal Statistical Society*, CXII, (1949), Part 2, pp. 207-23, and particularly in the important article by Rupert C. Jarvis, 'Official Trade and Revenue Statistics', *Economic History Review*, XVII, no. 1 (1964), pp. 43-62. Smuggling, the cause of so much distortion in the trade figures of certain series in the eighteenth century up to Pitt's reforms, may be initially introduced by W. A. Cole, 'Trends in Eighteenth Century Smuggling', *Economic History Review*, X, no. 3 (1958), pp. 395-410, whilst research into the customs organization of Liverpool may be represented by Rupert C. Jarvis, *Customs letter-books of the port of Liverpool, 1711-1813* (Manchester: Cheltenham Society, 1954). For the connection of the customs with national finance, the two works by Peter G. M. Dickson, *The Financial Revolution in England* (London: Macmillan, 1967) and John E. D. Binney, *British Public Finance and Administration, 1774-92* (Oxford: Clarendon Press, 1958) have no equals in nineteenth century studies.

The statistical record, which forms the main portion of the 1898 *Customs Report*, [C.8706] LXXV (IUP National Finance: General 8), has of course, been subjected to the same critical evaluation as the figures in the 1840 report, and they should be read in conjunction with authoritative revisionary works such as those of Albert H. Imlah, *Economic Elements in the Pax Britannica* (Cambridge, Mass.: Harvard University Press, 1958), and the same author's 'British Balance of Payments and the Export of Capital, 1816-1913', *Economic History Review*, V, no. 2 (1952), also Rupert C. Davis, 'Official Trade and Revenue Statistics', *Economic History Review*, XVII, no. 1 (1964). Other recent articles which qualify nineteenth century international trade statistics are Yehuda Don, 'Comparability of International Trade Statistics: Great Britain and Austria-Hungary before World War I', *Economic History Review*, XXI, no. 1 (1968) 78-92, and Robert E. Baldwin, 'Britain's Foreign Balance and the Terms of Trade', *Explorations in Entrepreneurial History*, V, no. 4 (1953), pp. 248-52.

Amongst the best general full-length works on British overseas trade covering the period of the later nineteenth century are Samuel B. Saul, *Studies in British Overseas Trade, 1870-1914* (Liverpool: The University Press, 1959), William Ashworth, *A Short History of the International Economy, 1850-1950* (London: Longmans, 1952), whilst Arthur L. Bowley's *A Short Account of England's Foreign Trade in the Nineteenth*

Century, revised ed. (London: Sonnenschein, 1905) is an excellent study from one of the free trade persuasion. An interesting comment on the work of diplomatic supporters of foreign trade outlets comes from D. C. M. Platt, 'The Role of the British Consular Service in Overseas Trade, 1825-1914', *Economic History Review,* XV, no. 3 (1963), pp. 494-512, and this may be read as an accompaniment to the *Appendix Part II* to the *Second Report from the Royal Commission on the Depression in Trade and Industry 1886,* 1886 [C.4715-1] XXII (IUP Trade and Industry: Depression 2).

For the early period of the national debt, the reader might well look at W. A. Shaw, 'The Beginnings of the National Debt', *Historical Essays by Members of Owens College, Manchester* (1902), pp. 391-422, and proceed to Alice C. Carter, 'The English Public Debt in the Eighteenth Century', *Historical Association Pamphlet,* H. 74, (1968). For the burden of the debt in that century see Charles Wilson and Alice C. Carter, 'Dutch Investment in Eighteenth Century England', *Economic History Review,* XXI, no. 3 (1960), pp. 434-48, which comprises two short articles, C. Wilson, 'Dutch Investment in Eighteenth Century England: A Note on Yardsticks', and an accompanying note by A. C. Carter, 'Note on a Note on Yardsticks', *Economic History Review,* XII, no. 3 (1960). These also refer the reader to the articles in *Economica,* New Series XX, (May 1953), pp. 159-61, and (November 1953), pp. 322-40, by Mrs Carter, The eighteenth century was of course, remarkable for its production of schemes for paying off the national debt, and only two mid-century examples are given here: Sir John Barnard, *Considerations on the Proposal for Reducing the Interest on the National Debt* (London: Osborn, 1750), and C. Robinson, *Considerations on the late Bill for Payment of Remainder of the National Debt, etc.* (Dublin: 1754). Two well-known examples in the early nineteenth century are: William Frend, *The National Debt in its True Colours* (London: 1817), and Richard Heathfield's *Elements of a Plan for the Liquidation of the National Debt* (London: 1820). A modern article which examines the role of the capital levy in this period is Manuel Gottlieb's 'The Capital Levy and Deadweight Debt in England, 1815-40', *Journal of Finance* (March 1953), pp. 34-46. Above all, the study by Eric L. Hargreaves, *The National Debt* (London: Cass, 1966) remains the general authority in this field of finance, though in parts the detail is too sparse for the specialist and may be supplemented by other secondary works. Other useful works for the later period of the debt are: Sidney Buxton, *Finance and Politics,* 2 vols (London: Murray, 1888), volume I being most useful, Sir Thomas Henry Farrer, *Mr Goschen's Finance: 1887-90* (London: Liberal Publication Dept., 1891), Sir Stafford H. Northcote, *Twenty Years of Financial Policy* (London: Saunders, 1862) and Sir Robert Giffen, *Essays in Finance,* 4th ed. (London: Bell, 1886). The Colwyn Report *(Report of the Committee on National Debt and Taxation),* 1927 Cmd. 2800, is worth close examination from the historical matter it contains, and the article by Olive Anderson 'Loans versus Taxes: British Financial Policy in the Crimean War', *Economic History Review,* XVI, no. 2 (1963), pp. 314-27, throws new light on this aspect of Gladstone's finance.

The place of the lottery in the history of the national debt has been

dealt with in several specialist studies. Amongst the earlier ones is John
Ashton, *A History of English Lotteries* (London: Leadenhall Press, 1893),
and more recent studies include R. D. Richards, 'The Lottery in the
history of English government finance', *Economic History*, III, no. 9
(January 1934), pp. 57-76, and Jacob Cohen, 'The Element of Lottery in
British Government Bonds, 1694-1919', *Economica*, New Series XX
(1953), pp. 237-46. The general works, P. G. M. Dickson, *The Financial
Revolution in England* (London: Macmillan, 1967) and J. E. D. Binney,
British Public Finance and Administration, 1774-92 (Oxford: Clarendon
Press, 1958) are so detailed that they inevitably give much valuable
information on this area of study. Finally, for comparative purposes, the
researcher should not neglect *Return of the National Debt of Great Britain
and Ireland, 1691-1857*, 1857-58 (443), XXXIII.

The case of Beaumont Smith lies wholly entombed in the 1842
Commissioners' Report on Forged Exchequer Bills and it is unlikely that
the historian will have great cause to disinter the bones of the scandal. The
writings of historians on the exchequer bill instrument, with the exception
of R. D. Richards', 'The Exchequer Bill in English Government Finance',
Economic History, III, no. 11 (February 1936), pp. 193-211, are to be
found exclusively in specialized works on government revenue raising, and
on the banking and money market sectors. In the first category should be
placed P. G. M. Dickson's *The Financial Revolution in England*, the most
authoritative and recent text on late seventeenth and early eighteenth
century government finance. To complement that work, J. E. D. Binney's
British Public Finance and Administration is an unrivalled exposition of
the pre-Napoleonic war era. Both works contain extensive references to
exchequer bills. The nineteenth century has not yet attracted studies of
comparative detail in this field. The best peripheral works, according to
the student's interest are: William M. Scammell, *The London Discount
Market* (London: Elek, 1968), E. Victor Morgan and W. A. Thomas, *The
Stock Exchange: its history and functions* (London: Elek, 1962), Thomas
S. Ashton and Richard S. Sayers, *Papers in English Monetary History*
(Oxford: Clarendon Press, 1953), and Sir John Clapham, *The Bank of
England: A History*, and Wilfrid Thomas C. King, *History of the London
Discount Market* (London: Routledge, 1936).

The most important specialized work on the history of expenditure
control is Basil Chubb's, *The Control of Public Expenditure* (Oxford:
Clarendon Press, 1952) and this has been joined more recently by Henry
Roseveare's study *The Treasury: the Evolution of a British Institution*
(London: Allen Lane, The Penguin Press, 1969). Both works, in their
respective fields, trace developments from their origins to the present day.
Only one modern full-length study deals with the period covered by the
select committee reports (IUP National Finance: 3, 4 and 5) and that is
Maurice Wright, *Treasury Control of the Civil Service, 1854-1874* (Oxford:
Clarendon Press, 1969). Wright's study contains much detail concerning
miscellaneous expenditure with summary tables of statistics of this
expenditure in his chosen period.

Paul Einzig's *The Control of the Purse* (London: Secker and Warburg,
1959) is a lively and authoritative general study written without the
impediments of scholarly references which the specialist demands. A

modern work which, though it provides numerous breakdown tables of
central and local expenditures mainly for the period from 1890, seeks to
trace the magnitude of government expenditures and relate these to the
growth of national income is that of Alan T. Peacock and Jack Wiseman,
The Growth of Public Expenditure in the United Kingdom (London: Allen
and Unwin, 1967), revised ed. *University of York Studies in Economics,*
no. 1. This study attempts to provide a framework for investigating the
springs of growth of government expenditures and it uses a particular
definition of expenditure categories to analyse the statistical riches of
British 'bluebooks'.

So important was the influence of nineteenth century financial
reformists in stirring parliament and the departments into action, in some
cases nearly to the borders of self-immolation, that biographical references
are not out of place even in a short bibliographical list. Some of the most
deserving of study are: Jennifer Hart, 'Sir Charles Trevelyan at the
Treasury', *English Historical Review,* LXXV, no. 294 (1960), pp. 92-110,
Andrew Lang, *Life, Letters and Diaries of Sir Stafford Northcote, First
Earl of Iddesleigh,* 2 vols (London: Blackwood, 1890), John Morley, *The
Life of William Ewart Gladstone,* 2 vols (London: Macmillan, 1905), Sir
Francis Baring, *Journals and Correspondence from 1808 to 1852,* ed. Earl
of Northbrook and Hon. Francis Baring (Winchester, 1902, 1905) and
Edmund Spencer E. Childers, *The Life and Correspondence of the Right
Hon. Hugh C. E. Childers, 1827-96,* 2 vols (London: Murray, 1901).

The details and history of Anglo-Irish financial relations are most
comprehensively contained in the text of IUP National Finance:
General 6, but these may be extensively supplemented by IUP Famine:
Ireland 1-8. For a modern overall view of economic policy towards Ireland
for most of the century see R. D. Collison Black, *Economic Thought and
the Irish Question, 1817-70* (Cambridge: Cambridge University Press,
1960). Gladstone's particular attitude in the later century is investigated in
John L. Hammond, *Gladstone and the Irish Nation* (London: Longmans,
1938) which discusses the basic political aspects of Irish land reform.

Author Index

Note: 79 in 76 refers to *footnote* 76 on page 79

Subject Index

Welby, 80
Wellington, Duke of, 17, 74
Westminster Review, 7
William III, 72
Wilson, James, 40

women, employment of, 2
Wood, Sir Charles, 40

Zollverein, 64 and n12, 66

Irish University Press publications

British Parliamentary Papers: subject-set arrangement

There are almost insurmountable difficulties in using the British parliamentary papers as they first appeared. Some five million pages in 7,000 volumes appeared between 1800 and 1925, the papers being bound in chronological order so that those on one subject are often spread through several hundred volumes.

For their thousand-volume reprint series, Irish University Press selected the key policy documents, including minutes of evidence, and arranged them into 82 subject-sets.

Area Studies sets covering British foreign relations in the period, including the United States of America, Russia, China and Japan, are also available.

All these volumes, averaging 640 pages, are available individually as well as by set and series.

British domestic and colonial affairs (1,000 volumes)

AGRICULTURE
General (32 volumes)
Animal Health (4 volumes)

ANTHROPOLOGY (3 volumes)

COLONIES
General (37 volumes)
Africa (70 volumes)
Australia (34 volumes)
Canada and Canadian Boundary (36 volumes)
East India (22 volumes)
New Zealand (17 volumes)
West Indies (10 volumes)

CRIME AND PUNISHMENT
Civil Disorder (8 volumes)
Juvenile Offenders (6 volumes)
Penal Servitude (2 volumes)
Police (10 volumes)
Prisons (21 volumes)
Transportation (16 volumes)

EDUCATION
General (46 volumes)
British Museum (4 volumes)
Fine Arts (6 volumes)
Poorer Classes (9 volumes)
Public Libraries (2 volumes)
Scientific and Technical (8 volumes)

EMIGRATION (28 volumes)

FAMINE, Ireland (8 volumes)

FISHERIES (7 volumes)

FUEL AND POWER
Coal Trade (5 volumes)
Gas (6 volumes)
Mining Accidents (12 volumes)
Mining Districts (2 volumes)
Mining Royalties (3 volumes)

GOVERNMENT
Civil Service (12 volumes)
Diplomatic Service (4 volumes)
Elections (5 volumes)
Municipal Corporations (9 volumes)

HEALTH
  General (17 volumes)
  Food and Drugs (5 volumes)
  Infectious Diseases (13 volumes)
  Medical Profession (5 volumes)
  Mental (8 volumes)

INDUSTRIAL RELATIONS
  (44 volumes)

INDUSTRIAL REVOLUTION
  Children's Employment
    (15 volumes)
  Design (4 volumes)
  Factories (31 volumes)
  Textiles (10 volumes)
  Trade (5 volumes)

INSURANCE, Friendly Societies
  (10 volumes)

INVENTIONS (2 volumes)

LEGAL ADMINISTRATION
  General (16 volumes)
  Criminal Law (6 volumes)

MARRIAGE AND DIVORCE
  (3 volumes)

MILITARY AND NAVAL
  (6 volumes)

MONETARY POLICY
  General (12 volumes)
  Commercial Distress (4 volumes)
  Currency (8 volumes)
  Decimal Coinage (2 volumes)
  Joint Stock Banks (1 volume)
  Savings Banks (4 volumes)

NATIONAL FINANCE
  General (8 volumes)
  Income Tax (2 volumes)

NEWSPAPERS (2 volumes)

POOR LAW (30 volumes)

POPULATION (25 volumes)

POSTS AND TELEGRAPHS
  (8 volumes)

RELIGION (3 volumes)

SHIPPING, Safety (9 volumes)

SLAVE TRADE (95 volumes)

SOCIAL PROBLEMS
  Drunkenness (4 volumes)
  Gambling (2 volumes)
  Sunday Observance (3 volumes)

STAGE AND THEATRE
  (3 volumes)

TRADE AND INDUSTRY
  Depression (3 volumes)
  Explosives (2 volumes)
  Navigation Laws (2 volumes)
  Silver and Gold Wares
    (2 volumes)
  Tobacco (2 volumes)

TRANSPORT (22 volumes)

URBAN AREAS
  Housing (3 volumes)
  Planning (10 volumes)
  Sanitation (7 volumes)
  Water Supply (9 volumes)

INDEXES
  General (8 volumes)
  Special (1 volume)

Area Studies

United States of America (60 volumes); Russia (38 volumes); China (42 volumes); Japan (10 volumes). Papers covering both China and Japan are included in the China set.

Bibliographical aids

Breviates and Select Lists

P. and G. Ford:
> *A Guide to Parliamentary Papers*, Shannon 1972
> *Select List of British Parliamentary Papers, 1833-99*, Shannon 1969
> *A Breviate of Parliamentary Papers, 1900-16*, Shannon 1969
> *A Breviate of Parliamentary Papers, 1917-39*, Shannon 1969

P. and G. Ford and Diana Marshallsay:
> *Select List of British Parliamentary Papers, 1955-64*, Shannon 1970

A Maltby:
> *The Government of Northern Ireland 1922-72. A catalogue and breviate of parliamentary papers*, Shannon 1973

Alphabetical Indexes

The eight-volume general alphabetical index of titles to nineteenth-century British parliamentary papers are part of the 1,000-volume series above.

Subject Indexes

New indexes to subjects, names and places in the IUP parliamentary papers are in preparation. There will be approximately 30 volumes of indexes, the first three of which will be published in 1973.

Checklist

Checklist of British Parliamentary Papers in the Irish University Press 1,000-Volume Series, 1801-99, Shannon 1972. This checklist supplements the general indexes; it contains chronological and alphabetical lists of all the papers in the IUP series together with a 'key-word index' of major specific subjects.

Monographs

P. Ford: *Social Theory and Social Practice*, Shannon 1968.

Commentaries

Information on further titles in the *Government and Society in Nineteenth-century Britain* series is available from Irish University Press on request.